# 5 Keys: How to go from Stress to Success

Daniel Spacagna

Life On Purpose Publishing
WINDSOR, CONNECTICUT

# 5 Keys: How to go From Stress to Success

Daniel Spacagna

All Rights Reserved
Copyright © 2016 by **Daniel Spacagna**

Cover Design © 2016 by **Daniel Spacagna**

Edited by **Dr. Angela D. Massey**

Printed in the United States of America. Except as permitted under the United States Copyright Act of 1976, no part of this publication may be reproduced, distributed or transmitted in any form or by any means, including photocopying, recording, or other electronic or mechanical methods, without the prior written permission of Daniel Spacagna, except in the case of brief quotations embodied in critical reviews and certain other noncommercial. For permission requests, write to the author, addressed "Attention: Permissions Coordinator," at the address below.

Daniel Spacagna
195 Union Street
Cleveland, OH 44146
www.danspacagna.com

All brand names and product names used in this book are trademarks, registered trademarks, or trade names of their respective holders.

This publication is designed to provide accurate and authoritative information in regard to the subject matter covered. It is sold with the under-standing that neither the publisher nor the author is engaged in rendering legal or other professional services. If legal advice or other expert assistance is required, the services of a competent professional person should be sought.

—From a declaration of principles jointly adopted by a committee of the American Bar Association and a committee of publishers.

A Gap Closer ™ Publication
    A Division of Life On Purpose Publishing
    Windsor, Connecticut

Ordering Information:
Quantity sales. Special discounts are available on quantity purchases by corporations, associations, and others. For details, contact the "Special Sales Department" at the address above.

**Five Keys From Stress to Success/ Daniel Spacagna.** —1st ed.

ISBN 978-0-9961908-6-2

# Contents

*Introduction* .................................................................... ix

The Operating System of Our Lives ................................. 1

Perception ............................................................................ 23

Interpretation ...................................................................... 45

Emotion ................................................................................ 61

Behavior ............................................................................... 85

Beliefs: The Master Key .................................................. 113

The Three P's ..................................................................... 129

*Acknowledgements*

I wish to thank the following people for their continuing love and support.

Thank you for always believing in me and encouraging me to go after my dreams:

- My wife, Lori Spacagna
- My mom, Sharon Spacagna
- My children: Samuel, Jaime and Joseph
- Jim and Boots (late) Hvisdos
- Joe and Joy Milano.

In words and deed you have encouraged me through thick and thin.

Thank you to the following individuals who, without their contributions to my personal and professional development, this book would not have been written:

- Pete Spacagna (brother)
- Adam Spacagna (brother)
- Keith New
- Sandy Ramirez
- Jaime Swindell
- Pastor Dave Brunelle
- Mike Hopkins

# Introduction

You know few things in life are inevitable, but pain is one of them. The truth is you're either in a painful season right now, just coming out of a painful season, or heading into a painful season. I now know that pain is inevitable, and I also now know that suffering stress is optional.

## From Pain to Purpose

You see, as a middle child of divorced parents, my life had its painful moments. Some pains were immediately apparent and others were more repressed. Growing up, I was the skinny, bucktoothed, straight-A student in grade school who couldn't do a chin-up to save his life. I heard name-calling like "nerd" or "wimp," nearly every day. I won't tell you about the bus rides home; they were especially brutal. I used to walk long routes to avoid bullies and avoid certain parts of the playground for fear of physical harm. Somehow, despite the fear of bullies, I managed to get straight-A's, that is until high school. My low self-esteem and fear caused me to drop all honor classes, and enter a vocational education program which allowed me to leave school early and destroyed any chance for a college scholarship.

As a young adult, I experienced my own divorce. I worked for my family business, doing contracting work which I really despised. I experienced all the ups and downs of work and family being connected.

No pain in my early life, though, prepared me for the sudden death of my co-worker and cousin at only 21 years old. This would then be followed by the death of my 33-year-old brother-in-law who had recently found the love of his life, purchased an engagement ring. He died a month later.

In my late 20s, I began experiencing debilitating pains, digestive disorders, clinical depression, jaw pain, allergies, and a myriad of other physical and psychological symptoms. I couldn't eat without experiencing massive pain, so I lived on ginger ale and saltine crackers for almost two years. I lost over 65 pounds and feared the worst. I finally went to the doctor. After weeks of uncomfortable tests, pokes and prods, my healthcare provider seemed helpless. His only solution was to prescribe drugs, which just masked the symptoms. I remember asking my doctor at one point, "What are the drugs fixing?" All he could tell me was, "They'll make you feel better." And I said, "Well beer makes me feel better, but that's not a solution." I couldn't accept living on drugs for the rest of my life.

One Saturday evening, I came to the end of my rope, and I was willing to let go. Life seemed hopeless, and I felt helpless. I kept getting hollow advice and clichés from friends and relatives. People told me, "Just snap out of it. Be happy." At that point, I had remarried, and we had a newborn child, and a condominium. Life was supposed to be great; right? However, it was when I told my wife I had lost the will to live that I hit bottom. I knew I could not survive mentally, or even physically, much longer.

## Express or Suppress

We have two options when it comes to the emotions we experience with pain or loss: We can express our emotions or suppress them. If we choose to suppress them, our mind, body, and spirit react in predictable ways. Suppressing emotions leads to depression, which then becomes some sort of disease and leads to physical, mental and emotional disintegration.

The flowchart for suppression is circular in nature as demonstrated in the following diagram.

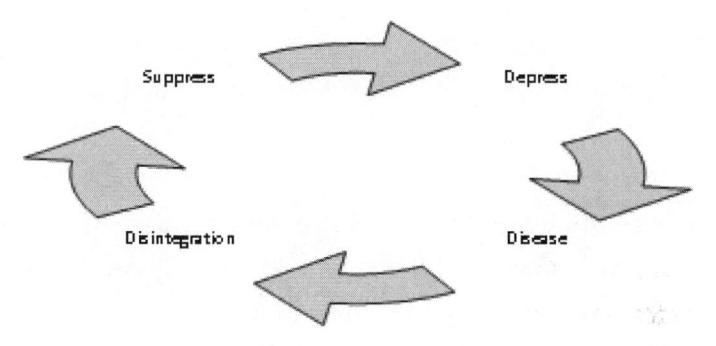

Suppress → Depress → Disease → Disintegration → (Suppress)

The diagram represents a process many people unknowingly create. I know this because an estimated 77% of Americans experience physical symptoms caused by stress. These symptoms include fatigue, headaches, upset stomach, muscle tension, loss of appetite, dizziness and more.

The American population represents only 5% of the world, yet annually, we consume over 85% of the world's prescription drugs. Using drugs to manage symptoms is comparable to having a "Check Engine" light on in your automobile and putting a piece of tape over it. You're not fixing anything with the tape; you're just masking the warning that you have a problem. The "Check Engine" light is not the problem; it's an indication of a problem. Your headaches, stomach aches, back pain, depression, anxiety, allergies, high blood pressure—that may be your "Check Engine" light. They are a warning that there is a system error somewhere else. Many times the presence of pain is not the problem but rather an indication of a problem.

Well, I'm here to tell you that you have choices. Suppressing symptoms and using drugs to interfere with symptoms doesn't fix anything. This program will give you techniques you can implement immediately to change your life. You can be free.

One day in my life, everything changed. I prayed for wisdom and knowledge, and my prayer was answered. A friend shared some truths with me and gave me some books to read. The interesting thing was my problems and the problems facing the world were the same, but I now had the tools to process problems differently. I found out I could look at the same situations and problems that previously triggered physical pain, psychological symptoms and negative emotions and I could choose a different pathway. It's like programming your navigation system with a destination using *Google* maps. I love *Google* maps because it automatically creates the fastest route. What's really great is when the computer sees slow traffic or an accident on your route, it will offer an alternative.

## The Navigation System to Happiness

I found my navigation system to create happiness, peace, and health. It took me years of reading and learning to find the truth. Once I got a taste of what was possible, I couldn't get enough. I read every book on psychology, emotional intelligence and success. I read all the best self-esteem books. I spent an entire week in the study of ancient writings and modern science. I paid for coaching programs and seminars. What I found is they all have common denominators, but they can be confusing to understand. I spent eight days in the desert, in prayer and meditation. I fasted for days, spent days in solitude and practiced silence.

Some things worked well and others did not. I found out it's like a combination lock. Do you remember the combination lock in high school the first year you had one? You were so nervous to get those numbers in the right order, because it you get the sequence out of order, you were not going to unlock the locker.

The same is true with emotional health, stress, and pain. You could hear some clichés and some truths about psychology and how the brain works, but if you don't put the numbers in the right order, you're not going to get the change. I have gathered the core truths from thousands of hours of research and put the steps in the right order to make it as easy for you as following a GPS.

Sometimes people experience different breakthroughs randomly through experiences. But I'm here to show you how to find the alternate route when life's incidents and accidents blindside you. I'll show you how there are alternate routes in every situation, routes to help you avoid the potholes of anger, the traffic jams of fear, and the closed road of depression. What's more? I've discovered that if you know how to adjust your course, the pain will bring you to your ultimate purpose in life. That's right. In fact, the more failures and losses you've gone through up until now, the better. Think of this way: the more pain, the more power, and ultimately, the most purpose.

Once I knew the combination, everything changed. The pain and depression left, and I could eat anything. I had the ability to take on any challenge that came my way. It led to multiple promotions and to leadership and management positions. My income doubled twice in just a couple of years. I am now fulfilling my purpose, and I have committed my life 100% to share these truths with people all over the world. You see I prayed for wisdom and knowledge and I promised if I figured this out, I would share it with anyone who asks me. This book is a fulfillment of a promise.

To date, I've spoken in nearly every state in the United States and all across Canada. Tens of thousands of people have attended my seminars and I have students from over 50 countries around the world via the Internet. I'm helping change people's lives by making psychology and emotional health as easy as following *Google* maps.

I want to share the five steps with you and they go like this – perception leads to interpretation which leads to emotion which creates behavior. The fifth step is the secret ingredient not taught in most psychology and self-help books, but don't peek ahead! You need to understand the foundation and the first four steps to operate the combination lock of your emotions successfully.

What Apple did for the smartphone, I want to do for psychology and personal change. I want to make it simple, easy-to-use and accessible for anyone at any age. At the end of each chapter, there are practical action items or to-dos. I like to think of these as preventive maintenance items for a healthy mind, body, and spirit. By the end of this book, you will be able to control your emotions in any stage of life. You'll be able to find true peace, true happiness and ultimately operate in the center of your purpose.

Are you ready? Let's get started.

Daniel Spacagna
Cleveland, Ohio

CHAPTER ONE

# The Operating System of Our Lives

*"You don't have a soul. You are a soul. You have a body."* Author Unknown

*"What the brain is to the body, the mind is to the soul."* Daniel Spacagna

*"As a man thinketh in his heart so is he."* Proverbs 23:7

To have the best opportunity to turn our pains and our emotions into purpose, we have to understand the operating systems of our lives. An operating system is commonly used in a computer and it's what separates a Macintosh from a Windows PC. While they both have the same hardware or the same processor, it's the computer's operating system that determines whether it's a Windows computer or an Apple computer.

Your brain is the hardware, but your mind is the operating system. To understand the mind we have to understand two basic functions: the cortex and the limbic. The cortex is commonly called the conscious part of your brain. The frontal cortex is where we keep logic, facts, awareness, and structure; the cortex values information. The limbic system is commonly called the unconscious or the subconscious; it doesn't value logic, facts, awareness and structure. In fact, limbic functions are automatic and most of the time you're not aware of their functions. They don't really change based on information. They change on based on history and repetition. They create comfort zones and drive emotion.

Let's separate behaviors and thoughts. Out of all the things you do every day while you're awake, what percentage of them do you think are driven by the logical part of your brain? What percentage of what you do is driven by the cortex versus the limbic? Would you be shocked to know that only about a third of what you do while you're awake is driven by the conscious part of your brain? Essentially, over two-thirds of what you do is an automatic limbic unconscious behavior.

There are different levels of unconsciousness. When you start to fall asleep, you go into alpha, then beta and so on, all the way into REM. However, assuming you're fully asleep, you're 100% unconscious. In fact, when you're asleep you still have dreams. You still have images in your mind but you're fully unconscious.

So what happens when you're awake? What about your thoughts? What percentage of your thoughts do you think are driven by the cortex or the conscious factual structured part of your brain? What part is driven by the limbic or the emotional, automatic, knee-jerk and repetitive-driven part of your brain? Would you be shocked to know that 85% of what you think while you're awake is automatic? It's driven by the limbic. No wonder people find it difficult to change! No wonder they don't understand how to get rid of bad habits. No wonder many parents struggle with their children's behavior. It's not driven by logic.

We're going to use the terms conscious, unconscious, cortex, and limbic interchangeably. In ancient writings, they would be called your heart. In Eastern religions it might be called your chakra or your chi. Christians might call it your soul, spirit, or your innermost being. Again, what the brain is to your body, the mind is to your spirit—to your unconscious, to your soul, your innermost being. In America we commonly say, "I love you with all my heart," and this is unusual to other cultures. Another culture would say, "I love with all of my stomach." Whether you say stomach or heart, the point is you're saying your innermost being, the unconscious part, the emotional part—the part that drives 85% of your thoughts.

Since 85% of what you think and over two-thirds of what you do is automatic, there's no logic in it. For example, think about driving home from work. You repeatedly drive the same route. Have you ever planned to run an errand after work and you begin your route home and the next thing you know you're home and you didn't stop and do your errand? What happened? Well, the unconscious part of your brain knew to drive home at five o'clock. It didn't know to run an errand; even though you wanted to stop, you didn't.

Or what about moving? Have you ever moved and kept the same job? So, you move your residence to another part of town but you keep the same job. If I called you and asked, "Hey, are you moving this weekend?" If you were, you would obviously say, "Yes, I'm moving." So you move all your stuff on the weekend. Now, imagine it's Sunday night and you all of your stuff is in boxes. You've left out only what you plan to wear to work on Monday. Let me ask you something, on Monday night, after work at five o'clock, where do you drive home to? Do you drive home to your new house? Or do some of you drive home to your old house even though you know you don't live there anymore?

This can happen with repetitive behaviors like speeding. I had 11 points on my driver's license early in my twenties. Every time I got pulled over for speeding I was not in a hurry. The officer would say, "What's the hurry, young man?" I would say, "I'm not in a hurry. I just didn't see you or I would have slowed down." Well, I had trained my subconscious to drive 10 to 15 miles above the speed limit. So even when I was not in a hurry, my unconscious brain was operating to do what I trained it to do.

I want you to understand that your unconscious brain is operating most of your life. Some people have affects with alcohol that makes them go unconscious and into a binge moment where they black out. An alcohol-induced blackout doesn't mean they necessarily pass out. Many people in such a blackout continue to party and hang out, but they're fully unconscious. In fact, the next day you could show them pictures on your Smartphone of what they did and they would not recollect any of it. They were fully blacked out; however, their eyes were open and they were dancing and doing whatever they do.

## How Neurological Loops Form

Consider this one example of how NASA discovered the 30-day principle for changing a behavior. NASA wanted to disorient their astronauts to see how they would react and if they would be able to operate the equipment under stress. Would they get nauseous? Would they struggle to fly the simulator? They wanted a controlled experiment on earth to prepare the astronauts for the worst-case scenario. They decided to replace the goggles of the astronauts with inverted-lens goggles so that the lenses were convex, because wearing convex lenses inverts your perception. The astronauts had to wear these goggles and operate the simulators and do everything they would normally do throughout the day. To get the full effect, the astronauts were told to keep the goggles on 24 hours a day, seven days a week. So, when they put these goggles on, their vision would become inverted: the floor would appear on the ceiling, and the ceiling would appear on the floor. Everything was upside down. They were then instructed to perform their normal daily functions: operate their simulators, eat breakfast and lunch, etc. Imagine trying to eat breakfast with everything inverted. Your food appears up on the ceiling so your motor reflexes will reach up when it's down and down when it's up.

NASA discovered that after about 24 to 25 days, some of the astronauts' brains corrected the image. So, even though they were getting the upside-down ocular image—automatically and without will power—their brain subconsciously flipped the image. By day 30, every single astronaut's brain corrected the image. NASA concluded that it takes about 24 to 30 days to get your brain to create a new neurological loop.

They did a subsequent experiment that is as equally interesting. They took a new group of astronauts, put the goggles on them and said, "Start doing your normal process." After 15 days, they instructed half of the group to take the goggles off for one day. After 24 hours, the astronauts were instructed to put the goggles back on. Interestingly enough, every astronaut who left the goggles on got the flip by day 30, because like before their brains corrected the image. However, none of the astronauts who interrupted the cycle got the change. The astronauts were then instructed to leave the goggles on for 30 consecutive days after they took the break. It took them about 45 days to get that flip. Why? When you're creating a new neurological loop in your unconscious, if you interrupt the cycle, you revert back to the old pattern.

You can think of neurological loops or unconscious loops or patterns as train tracks. Once you're on a set of tracks the only way to get the train off the tracks is to switch the points. The challenge when you're creating habitual unconscious emotional behaviors is the urge to switch the points to a new pattern for a weekend, perhaps. However, on Monday, if you go back to the old pattern and you switch the points back, it will just default to that permanently. In other words, you lose all the work you did in creating the new behavior, and like the astronauts you have to start all over again.

One of my favorite teachings about the conscious and unconscious is a teaching called *The Horse and The Rider*, created by psychologist, Dr. Tom Miller. He compared the brain, the conscious and unconscious to someone riding a trail horse.

I don't know if you've ever ridden a trail horse or been on one. I did it one time and didn't really have that great of an experience. I was a city kid who had never been on a horse. I didn't know the routines, but I was still excited. I thought, "Hey, I watched Bonanza growing up. This should be fun!" So I had all these visions of grandeur where I would get to gallop and pretend I was shooting things and splash through the streams, etc. I soon discovered it was nothing like what I envisioned.

I was dating my wife then and I thought it would be romantic—maybe Luther Vandross would be up in a tree singing to us. It wasn't like that at all! I was a little bit alarmed early on when I received no instructions on how to steer the horse. I don't know if that's the right term. I don't know if you steer a horse or not. But, I received no instructions; I found out about an hour and a half later that I didn't need any. The reason I needed no instructions was because I was not in control of the horse; the horse was in control of the horse! That horse was going to walk the trail no matter what I did.

It was disappointing for me because I thought I would have more control. I felt like a child at an amusement park when you put him or her in one those old-fashioned cars. Remember the simulated old-fashioned cars? The child thinks he or she is steering but the steering wheel is not attached to anything. It's running on a track but the child doesn't know that. So, he or she is experiencing all the excitement of driving a car, even though that is not reality. That's how I felt. I thought, "You're not getting me. I'm not driving this horse. I'm not steering. This horse is going to walk the path no matter what I do." In fact, they could have put me on this horse backwards and it would have still successfully navigated the course.

How many people do you know who want to go one direction in their life but all their behaviors go in the opposite direction? You see, about two hours into the ride I got a little aggressive with my horse because I thought, you know what, I'm getting this horse off the trail for a minute. I saw a shortcut I wanted to take where we could splash through a stream and fulfill *some* of my fantasy. So, when I got to that point in the trail, I pulled the reins as hard as I could and did my most aggressive Bonanza "Yee-haw!" What's interesting is the horse's head turned right but his body continued to go left. That's how so many people are living. They say, they want to be happy, healthy and wealthy, but all of their actions are programmed to get what they've always gotten. They say they want to have a relationship and get married one day but they've never meet anybody. They don't talk to anybody. They say, they want to be debt-free, yet they continue to spend money they don't have.

## Information vs. Transformation

We don't need information—cortex—rider information. We need unconscious heart work and transformation. So, who's controlling your life? It's not the rider. It's the horse. Did you know you had a horse? Did you know that you're responsible for training your horse? If you don't train your horse, your horse will train you!

Another one of my favorite teachings is a process called E plus R equals O which means: Event plus Response equals Outcome. In the work of psychology and emotional intelligence, the feeling of being out of control in your life is one of the sources of stress. When you feel out of control in your finances, you get stressed. When you feel out of control with your health, you get stressed. When you feel out of control with your children you get stressed. You have to know what you can control and what you cannot control.

## E + R = O

The event plus your response determines the outcome. What most people do is when they don't get the outcome they want in a situation, they blame the event. They blame the weather, the government, their parents, their boss, the product they've been given, their territory, another employee's behavior, etc. What the experts in human behavior recommend is if you really want to have more success in life, you have to own your response because the events are probably not going to change. You have to change the way you think. You have to change the pictures in your mind. You have to change your behaviors. You have to change your beliefs, and then you can start producing better outcomes.

What do you have control over today? Can you change events in the past? No, you can't change events in the past. They happened, and they're over. So that is a low control area. How about outcomes? Can you guarantee and control outcomes? Do you have control over your outcomes? Well, there are some outcomes that are inevitable like death. But you don't know when it will happen, do you? You can live healthy and move to the suburbs, but that doesn't guarantee you will live a long life. The reality is you have low control over the outcome and low control over the events. What do you have 100% control of? You have 100% control of your ability to respond. So, take 100% responsibility—no blaming, no complaining—take control.

The minute you blame and complain, you give the only area of power you had to someone else. When it comes to blaming and complaining, I think I've heard it all. "I'm not coming to work on time because my co-worker doesn't come to work on time." Great! Now, your co-worker is in control of your attendance. No blaming. No complaining.

The average American spends several hours on social media. Ponder this: is social media positive or negative? Is social media creating an accurate perception of reality or is it focusing only on the worst events and behaviors of society? Shut off your social media for a month and watch what happens in your brain.

What if you did a 30-day no blaming and complaining challenge at work? Some of your co-workers would probably not speak for a month because all they do is blame and complain! Again, when you blame and complain you train yourself to give up the only power you have; take 100% responsibility for everything in your life. Besides, most of it you created, promoted, or allowed to keep happening. Control your response. Control your decisions. Influence your attitude. Influence your unconscious. You can influence other people and influence outcomes by owning your response.

Now, if your doctor gave you a prescription for an ear infection—we've all had an ear infection, and we have had to take a prescription for two weeks; right? Would you want your body to respond to the medicine or react to the medicine? No, you don't want to have a reaction. You want your body to respond to the medicine. And people who are highly unconscious react to events and they blame their reaction on the events.

One approach to E+R=O is to reverse engineer your life. In other words, identify the outcome you want and back into the response that creates that outcome. The painful events in your life are just that, events; the outcome has not been determined. The ability to respond is your high position of power. Ask yourself regarding past events, "How could I have responded differently to create different outcomes?" Listen, if you're on the right side of the dirt—that means if you're alive—then your outcome is not set in stone. There's still a chance. Choose the response that creates the outcome you want.

What if you're very reactive? Let's talk about how your horse was trained to be reactive. The best way to make this point is to ask, "Can people make you mad? Can I make you mad? Can your mother-in-law make you mad? Can your co-workers make you mad? Yes or no?" What do you think? Can people make you mad? Now, most people will say, "Well, sure, Dan, you could do unkind things to me. You could be rude, and that would make me mad." But the reality is no one can make you mad. Why? *Your* brain is attached to *your* spinal cord; *their* brain is attached to *their* spinal cord! Really, it's that simple. Emotion or anger is created in your brain. No one has Bluetooth on it yet. I say *yet* because who knows? With the way technology is going they might! But right now no one else can control your brain. You make yourself feel anything you feel. Your unconscious programming may create patterns that cause you to react negatively but it's your brain. If events always made us feel a certain way, they would always work.

Imagine some of the things that upset you at work: someone coming in late on a busy Monday or angry customers raising their voices, etc. Or someone leaving the printer jammed without saying anything about it. If you change one thing in any of those scenarios, the events become meaningless. Imagine you give your two weeks' notice because you have this new career that doubles your income. It's a promotion, maybe a management position you've wanted for ten years. You've finally gotten it. You give your two weeks' notice at work. Now imagine it's the Friday of your last two weeks. Got it? On that Friday, someone comes in late or a customer raises his or her voice or someone leaves the printer jammed—would you get as mad as you would have before? Probably not, because if those things made you feel mad they would always make you feel mad. If your emotional response changed because of your new job, then it wasn't the event that caused your anger. It's coming from somewhere else in your unconscious.

The reality is you may have an unconscious reaction to something else. You're not even aware of why you're mad, but we are trained to blame other people. At the risk of being offensive, the truth is if you are irritated by idiots, you're probably the idiot! Here's what I mean, what if I accused you of having blue hair? Of course, I can't see you, so maybe you do have blue hair, but let's assume you don't. Maybe you're a brunette, or you have brown hair, or you have blond hair. So if I accused you of having blue hair, would that bother you? Probably not; right? Why? Because you know that you don't have blue hair. You might even say, "Dan, I don't know what you're talking about." You might be concerned that maybe the lighting is bad, but you wouldn't get defensive or feel hurt because you *know* it's not true. If someone calls you a thief, it can only bother you if you believe it's true.

## Cognitive Dissonance

There's something in our brain called *cognitive dissonance* or structural tension. Advertisers use it to motivate people to want their products. One example is if you've ever test-driven a brand new car, like one of the top of the line high-end cars. Maybe you went into the dealership for an oil change, and your Hyundai is paid off and you are fine with it. If I ask you logically, "Do you want a new car?" You would say, "No, I don't want a new car. I love my car."

Maybe the salesperson talks you into taking a test drive while you're waiting for the oil change on your Hyundai. He or she puts you in a Lexus high-end luxury top-of-the-line vehicle. While you're driving that Lexus, unconsciously you're feeling things. For example, the seat feels better and the steering is tighter. It smells better and the sound system is great. When you're done with the test drive, you're still in a logical frame of reference. You're saying, "No. I don't want a 72-month car payment. I'm good." So you get your old Hyundai back when the oil change is done. As soon as you sit down in your car and pull out of the parking lot, structural tension or cognitive dissonance begins. It's that feeling of dissatisfaction now that you're in your own car. You now notice how the seat is not very comfortable. You now notice all the squeaks and rattles. Once you create structural tension or cognitive dissonance, if you remain in it long enough one of two things will happen, you will either stop test driving the Lexus or you'll buy one. You can't keep sitting in really high-end cars and still feel comfortable with your old Hyundai.

Advertisers create cognitive dissonance to get you motivated to upgrade your cellphone or computer or get the latest technology. Apple is one of the best at this. If you go into an Apple store, they put everything out on tables. They want you to try that iPhone, to touch it, to feel it, to see how fast it is, to see how much brighter the screen is than yours. It's that cognitive dissonance that motivates people to spend double on an Apple product.

You know, if you want granite counter tops and you have the old Formica, all you have to do is hang around a friend who has granite counter tops and then cook at that friend's house every day or every week. You will either stop cooking at your friend's house or you will update your counter tops. I'm not saying granite counter tops are what you want; I'm just using it as another example of structural tension. Why not create structural tension for what you really want—for your purpose in life? Imagine if nothing less than happiness, fulfillment and purpose were comfortable for you.

There is a cognitive dissonance in our brains for being positive or negative. Your brain has only so much capacity for positive and negative storage. What's really challenging is how you can affect the positive to negative ratio. Consider this fuel tank analogy to understand the capacity ratios. Let's say the positive part of your brain has a fuel tank capacity of 20 gallons, and the negative part of your brain has a fuel tank capacity of 80 gallons. You have nearly four times the capacity to store negativity than you do positivity! That is why the media defaults to fear-based programming. It gets better results. If you're automatically reacting negatively to situations and events, let me suggest that you have not put much into the positive tank. You only have a 20 gallon capacity which means if you're a very busy person—if you're in leadership or a busy parent and are married—you need to stop constantly for positive fuel or your brain will default to the negative. So, it's 20 gallons to 80. Create cognitive dissonance for what you want. To train your brain to run on positivity, you may need to top off the positive side every hour or so. Eventually your unconscious will default to look for the positive automatically.

## Dealing with Loss

"They lost everything!" Often this is the statement quoted about a family that lost their home in a fire, a natural disaster or similar incident where their home and possessions were destroyed. This statement is uttered while a picture of the family is displayed on the news or other media outlets. It drives me crazy when people say this. They lost *nothing*. How do I know this? I know this because the family is pictured, healthy and alive. Health is everything. Life is everything.

They lost some shingles, some two by fours and drywall. I can hear you saying, "Yeah, but what about their memories?" Their memories are in their mind which they still have! One of the reasons people go "numb" when they lose their house is because that's where they have invested all of their time, money and focus. Their unconscious horse believes the house and the stuff is everything they have. This is so sad.

You can convince your brain otherwise. You can face adversity without a mental breakdown. You can find peace in the midst of losses. About a year ago, Joelle and Ryan who are friends of mine experienced the sudden loss of their home and possessions in a house fire. With their permission, I want to share their immediate and raw response to the situation as they expressed gratitude in the midst of the loss.

"UPDATE:

> *Thank you from the bottom of our hearts for the love and support that has been showered on our family. We are doing well. People keep asking why we aren't more upset. First, the Lord is amazing and provides peace for the storm. Secondly, 5 years ago we lost our sister-in-law and niece in a tragic car accident. It still brings immediate tears to my eyes. It was devastating and still hurts. And it brings perspective. It's hard to lose all your worldly possessions. But it's infinitely easier than losing the people you walk through life with. I'm so, so thankful that my family was safe that every little bonus God gives us brings me great joy."*

Did you notice the dissonance Joell used to manage her stress? She compared the loss of some stuff to the loss of her sister-in-law and niece. In the midst of their loss of a home, they expressed gratitude. Pain and loss squeezes the sponge of our souls and expresses whatever we've been focusing on. What we have been absorbed in gets squeezed out when we experience loss.

Here is another poignant example:

> *Horatio Spafford was a wealthy Chicago lawyer with a thriving legal practice, a beautiful home, a wife, four daughters and a son. He was also a devout Christian and faithful student of the Scriptures. His circle of friends included Dwight L. Moody, Ira Sankey and various other well-knowns of the day.*
>
> *At the very height of his financial and professional success, Horatio and his wife Anna suffered the tragic loss of their young son. If that weren't enough and shortly thereafter on October 8, 1871, the Great Chicago Fire destroyed almost every real estate investment that Spafford had.*
>
> *In 1873, Spafford scheduled a boat trip to Europe in order to give his wife and daughters a much needed vacation and time to recover from the tragedy. He also went to join Moody and Sankey on an*

*evangelistic campaign in England. Spafford sent his wife and daughters ahead of him while he remained in Chicago to take care of some unexpected last minute business. Several days later he received notice that his family's ship had encountered a collision. All four of his daughters drowned; only his wife had survived. His wife notified him by telegraph with these words: Survived alone.*

*With a heavy heart, Spafford boarded a boat that would take him to his grieving Anna in England. It was on this trip across the same sea that had swallowed up his daughters, that he penned the now famous words:*

> *"When peace like a river, attendeth my way,*
>
> *When sorrows like sea billows roll*
>
> *Whatever my lot, thou hast taught me to say*
>
> *It is well, it is well, with my soul"*

## The Three T's: Time, Talent, Treasure

In the work of psychology the area where you spend your time, talent, and treasure convinces your brain that you mean business. None of us would drop a $20 bill on the ground and ignore it. Since we believe there is value in a $20 bill, we would stop and pick it up. Time, talent, and treasure are a gateway into our unconscious brain and the beginning of structural tension.

The more time we spend, the more conditioned our brains become. It changes our focus and what we focus on programs our unconscious. When we invest our talent for someone else's benefit we shift our focus off of ourselves and we begin to experience perpetual joy. We'll talk more about that a little bit later.

## Time

Create a discipline of repetition. Watch or listen to positive programs the first thing every morning. Remember, when you're asleep, you're fully unconscious. So, one of the life hack ways to get into your unconscious is first thing in the morning and the last thing at night. The first thing you do in the morning and the last thing that you do at night is a very fertile time to reprogram your brain. Your unconscious is like a garden. The garden doesn't tell you what to plant; it just returns what you planted. So make sure what you start and end your day with is positive and tied to what you want.

What do most people watch first thing in the morning and last thing at night? The news! Is the news mostly positive or mostly negative? Yes, it's almost all negative. Worry and stress are an automatic subconscious horse trail that believes all of these negative things are going to come true. Worry is using your imagination for the worst possible outcome. Start and end your day with what you want: positivity, faith, hope, love.

Use "I am" statements. "I am" statements are the most powerful words to the unconscious brain—the most powerful words to your horse.

*I am happy*

*I am free*

*I am more than a conqueror.*

Write down the responses to negative events you want to have.

## Talent

Create cognitive dissonance for what you want or against what you don't want. When it comes to relationships, you are the average of the people you spend the most time with. If seven out of eight of your friends are negative, out of shape, and fearful, then you are about to be the eighth. Surround yourself with people who have accomplished what you want to accomplish. Surround yourself with people who are what you want to be. You know how to be overweight, broke and negative. You don't need friends who enable this comfort zone.

> *"By the skillful and sustained use of propaganda, one can make a people see even heaven as hell or an extremely wretched life as paradise."* Adolf Hitler.

Remember this, repetition is more important than content. The average American spends four to six hours watching television with repeated commercials. They add an additional three to four hours of Facebook and social media and Internet time. Repetition is creating cognitive dissonance for what advertisers want you to want, for what the media wants you to want, for what your politicians want you to want. You have to tip the scales to your side. How? Find people who have overcome what you want to overcome. This could be in small groups, in meetings, etc. Find some achievers.

## Treasure

What you spend your money on convinces your brain that it's important to you. Watch online classes. Pay for training. Shut off cable for 90 days and take that money and invest it in some good information, literature, and seminars. Go on a retreat. Stop watching TV shows that don't edify your soul. Stop watching the news. The news is completely unnecessary. If something bad happens, you'll find it out because someone will be quick to tell you. You don't need to watch the news; besides, 92% of what happens on the news or what they tell you to worry about it never happens. It's mostly gossip and exaggerations to motivate you to watch another episode. Shut down the gossip. If you're not part of the problem or part of the solution, that's called gossip. You're convincing your brain to care about things that do not matter to you when you spend time engaging in gossip.

Invest in yourself and hire a coach. You know, one of the most uncomfortable things I ever did was to hire a coach; however, it convinced my brain that I was serious about going to the next level.

Have you ever heard of the *law of attraction?* Basically, it states you become what you think about. You literally draw and magnetize what you focus on. More accurately stated it is the law of vibrational energy. One of the most powerful ways to change your operating system is to change the energy in your life. Everything on earth has a vibrational energy to it such as the color orange and vitamin C; middle C and 440 C on a piano vibrate at the same frequency. When you continue to vibrate in a negative frequency you actually magnetize negative things towards you. So, focus on whatever is good, whatever is lovely, whatever is pleasing. Think about those things and you will draw more of them into your life.

What if your operating system were programmed with gratitude? What if you were attracting more positivity and peace instead of negativity and fear? The rest of this book will break down the five steps to fully install the operating system for success and purpose.

## Questions

- Do you spend more time focusing on positivity or negativity?

- If you were on trial and a jury had to convict you of your beliefs based on your checking account, what would the jury believe about you?

- Do you invest your time into anyone other than yourself?

# Stress to Success Action Steps

*Commit to at least one action item from Time, Talent, and Treasure before you move on to the next chapter! Make it stick!*

Time:

Talent:

Treasure:

CHAPTER TWO

# Perception

*"Change the way you look at things
and the things you look at change."* Wayne Dyer

*"Your perspective on life comes from
the cage you were held captive in."* Shannon Alder

*"The difference between average people and achieving people is their perception
of and response to failure."* John Maxwell

*"Everything that irritates us about others can lead
us to an understanding of ourselves."* C.G. Jung

There is a common mode of human behavior used in psychology called the *human behavior model*. I like to call it the flowchart of human behavior which consists of five steps. Step one is perception. Perception is what you think you saw, felt, heard or experienced. All sensory information is filtered and creates perception. Step two is your interpretation of what you think you saw, felt, heard or experienced. Step three is your emotion, which is driven by your interpretation. Step four is your behavior according to what you thought you felt and remember—this is mostly done subconsciously. Finally, step five is a special master key which unlocks and circumvents all the other steps.

Once you get to step five I will teach you how a special master key can unlock all the other steps. However, it's very important to understand how your brain actually creates behavior through emotion, interpretation and perception. Remember how the high school janitor had a special key that could open every locker? Your master key is going to function in the same way. It can change your behavior, your emotion, your interpretation, or your perception.

In any positive or negative event, before you feel any emotion, your senses experience the event. This experience creates your perception and the rule in psychology is your brain *and mine* does not know the difference between a real or a perceived event. So in the formula I introduced in the previous chapter, E+ R=O (event plus response equals outcome) events can be real or perceived. Have you ever been scared by nothing at all? You perceived a threat and all of your fight or flight emotions engaged. Again, real or perceived events create real emotions. This is a huge concept because positive or negative, your stress can be created from nothing at all. Perceived events trigger the same emotions as real events.

## Paradigms

Another way to look at this is that your perception is your paradigm. The first time I heard about paradigm I thought they were talking about 20 cents, you know, two dimes. That's not what a paradigm is! A paradigm is the filtering lens by which you experience life; it's the map of your life.

For instance, I grew up in the Great Lakes region in Cleveland, Ohio. My perception of the area is based on where the lake is located. Cleveland is right on Lake Erie, which is north of the city and north of Ohio. So, the only thing north of Cleveland is Lake Erie and then Canada. Essentially, there is no north side of Cleveland; no one ever uses that term. Let's imagine that I meet you and you're from Chicago and you grew up in a Great Lakes region but your lake is east of the city, so for you there is a north side of Chicago. Now, we might hit it off and have immediate rapport because of our common denominator—you're from a Great Lakes region and so am I. You have horrible weather, and so do I. You have a lot of cloud cover and overcast skies, and so do I. We have rapport; yet, we may not know why. It's because our paradigms are similar. The problem surfaces when you, being from Chicago, start referring to the north side of town. I wouldn't understand why you were saying that because for me there is no north side of town.

You see, I assume everybody's paradigm is exactly like mine. I assume their map is the same as mine; that's a huge mistake we make in life and in relationships. We assume that what we see is what everybody else sees. Let that sink in for a minute. In what ways has assuming that your reality is the same as everyone else's created relational, financial, spiritual, emotional and professional problems for you?

Early in the development of the Greater Cleveland area, there wasn't a freeway that connected the southeast suburbs to downtown. I have family members that always took Broadway Avenue to get downtown. Everyone knew you just head north on Broadway Avenue and eventually you would be in Cleveland. Broadway Avenue in the suburbs was only about 12 miles from downtown Cleveland. Since Broadway Avenue was a main street with lots of stop lights and cities, it would take probably close to an hour to get downtown taking this route. Some years later, when I started driving, they created an interstate system. I started taking the Interstate to get downtown. But the challenge was this: to get on the Interstate, you actually go away from the city instead of going north towards the city. Once you get out on the entrance ramp you actually drive about five more miles, but your time is cut in half because you're able to drive 70 miles per hour with no stop lights. I remember how weird it felt to go south on Broadway knowing I was heading to Cleveland. However, because I knew about the freeway I chose to go backwards for a few minutes to save many minutes.

I believe that's a great example of what many people experience in life—they don't understand how you could see it differently. They don't understand why you would go south if you want to go north. They cannot see how it is possible that you could express peace and joy in the midst of loss or how you could give to someone else during times of your own financial strain. Their map is incomplete.

We took a driving trip years ago with two friends. This was before navigational systems, Google maps, etc. We had an *AAA TripTik* for part of the trip, and we used some atlases and maps for part of the trip. So we got on the Interstate—we left Ohio and we were headed to Myrtle Beach. Myrtle Beach is on the East Coast in South Carolina and since I was driving, I started heading south. My friend said, "Dan, why are we going south? We want to go to the coast." You see, his perception was thrown off! His paradigm was that you go east to the ocean and then south. Now, that's true; it would have worked. It just would have turned our 11-hour road trip into a 16 or 17 hour road trip. I knew that we would avoid major cities and major traffic if we went south first, then east. However, that made no sense to my friend because he knew that we were headed to the coast. This is the point: if you're not getting the results other people are getting, maybe you're not using the best map! Maybe there's a shortcut that you're not aware of. Maybe you are too focused on your route and you are not able to comprehend or see another possibility.

## Reticular Activating Systems

The challenge with a paradigm is you have a filter on your brain that creates your perception. So, an event happens and you don't see or experience the event as it was. You experience, see, hear, and feel what your brain lets through the filter. The filter is called the R.A.S., or the reticular activating system. When I learned about this it absolutely changed my life.

The reticular activating system is a filter that blocks sensory content. So, you're not experiencing life as it is. You're experiencing life as your brain allows it. You're not hearing everything. You're not seeing everything. You're not feeling everything that's there. All sensory information is filtered. It's mostly an unconscious automatic filtering, and this filter is there to prevent your brain from sensory overload.

I like to call the reticular activating system the bouncer to the door of your brain—like the bouncer at a night club. The bouncer lets some people in, but he doesn't let all people in. He will probably only let in people who he believes he will be of benefit to their club. Your brain does the same thing. It's like a filter on your internet.

## Filters

In the most generic sense, what does a filter do? A filter blocks content. Before you judge *this* content by saying, "Well, Dan, the filter blocks bad stuff." I agree; that may be true and it may not be true. It's selective. Your internet filter at work might block *eBay* and *Craigslist* but those aren't necessarily evil websites. They're not bad websites. They're just not what your company wants you spending time on at work.

Your brain blocks content in the same way. Let me give you some examples. Have you ever been in a crowded place, maybe it's a party or a work function, and you hear someone say your first and last name out loud, across the room? You couldn't hear what they said about you, but you heard your name crystal clear. You know they said something about you. You're wondering, "Who is talking about me?" Have you ever wondered why you could hear your name but nothing else? It's because your name is programmed into your filter. Why? You've been hearing it since the day you were born. The repetition of your name and the importance associated with it programmed it into your brain.

My wife and I had our first child 16 years ago. When he was born, we lived in a home located in a noisy part of town. What is interesting is the first night we brought our son to our home with all the street traffic, and other noises, we could still hear any sound he made in the middle of the night. Was he louder than everything else? No. But for nine months we had been thinking about and focusing on the prospect of being parents. So, our filter did two things: one, it blocked information (the noises) and, two, it only let in what was programmed (the sounds of our son).

## A Closer Look at Perception

The first step to understanding your perception is this: what you focus on is what your brain will let in. What you focus on is what you'll see. For example, if you focus on fear, all you will experience is fear. Everything will create a fear response. Is it really the event that's creating it? No. It's your perception of the event. You believe that something bad is going on and that's all you see. Other people focus on hope and love, and no matter what happens that's all they see.

There are many ways to test your perception. One test has two tiles and when you look at the tiles, the bottom one looks white and the top looks black. The reality is they're both the same color, but your brain is making a subconscious perceptual choice to see them as different. Remember the blue or white dress picture on social media that went viral? Some people saw that dress as blue, some people saw it as white; that was the subconscious perceptual filtered reticular system slanting it.

Perhaps the most widely known perception experiment was conducted by Daniel Simons. Simons asks his audiences to observe a video of two teams of three people. There are six people total, and three are wearing white shirts. Three are wearing black shirts. Both "teams" have a kickball, and they bounce the ball and pass it to their teammates. Before the video starts he asked participants to count the number of passes between the players wearing white. So now there are two teams, both passing balls to their respective teammates. Somewhere in the middle of the video, a 6-foot-tall gorilla enters stage left, stops at center stage, beats his chest, and then exits stage right. I have played this video to large crowds and found that less than 20% see the gorilla. That's amazing! How could they miss a 6-foot-tall gorilla right in the middle of the room? The reason is in the short term they told their brain to focus on something else, "Count the passes between the players wearing white shirts," and their brain rejected or filtered out all the other information. It's called perceptual blindness. I have a link to Simon's video in the reference section of this book. You can test it yourself with your classes and your co-workers. Don't tell them about the gorilla and see if they notice it. Again, I found less than 20% will actually see the gorilla.

A few months ago, a company in Europe made a startling discovery. An employee stopped showing up to work six and a half years earlier. The company personnel didn't find out until a few months ago. The employee was disgruntled with management, and he just stopped showing up. What's interesting is they continued to pay him for six and a half years. The only way they found out was when they were going to give him an award for ten years of employment, and they couldn't find him. He wasn't there! He hadn't been there in nearly seven years, and no one noticed. You are not seeing, hearing, and feeling what is there. You're seeing, hearing, and feeling what your brain lets in.

## Money and Perception

Let me ask you, do you feel rich? Now, if someone had asked me that question 10 or 15 years ago, I would have said, "No way!" I was making about $25,000 a year, and I would have said, "No chance. I am poor. We're broke." There is a website called www.Globalrichlist.com where you can put the country that you live in and your income, and it will tell you where you rank financially in the world. Let me save you some time. If you make $25,000 US dollars per year, you're in the top two percent of wealth in the world. The fact is 98% of the people on earth right now live on less than $25,000 USD; 98% of the people on earth consider you rich. When you're dead and gone, and you're surrounded by a cloud of witnesses of people who lived on this earth, you'll be a two percenter. Did that knowledge make you feel rich? Let me suggest that your feelings don't come from facts. The fact is if you make $25,000 compared to the world, you're in the top two percent. If you make $50,000—I don't even want to tell you where that puts you—but if you go to the website, you'll find out you're somewhere in the top 0.50.03% based on income.

When I made $25,000, we lived check to check and were broke and had no savings. I thought, if I can only make $50,000 that would change everything. When I made $50,000, we lived on a 130 percent of my income, and we were in more debt than when I made $25,000. So then I thought, "You know what? Six figures is it!" Isn't that what everyone says, you make six figures and you've arrived at success? I began changing my pain to purpose and applying what I'm teaching you and what do you know? I made over $100,000. When I made six figures, we lived on 150 percent of our income because I had a higher credit score. We were in more debt when I made six figures than when I made $25,000. The problem wasn't my income; the problem was my perception of success and money.

## Fear and Perception

Do you feel safe? Would you say the world, and maybe even the United States, is less safe than it's ever been? Or is it about as safe as it's been in all of its history? Or is it safer? Now, the facts are, there are fewer deaths per capita due to social violence, wars and other kinds of violence than any other decade in history. If you don't feel safe, it's not the facts that create your feelings of insecurity. It's your perception. If you're in the habit of watching the morning and nightly news, you probably don't feel safe because the media takes one bad event and talks about it for 90 days over and over and replay it thousands of times. Alternatively, if you're glued to social media, then every time someone treats someone poorly, and it's replayed a million times, the repetition will affect your perception. You will start to see the world as a violent place and in fact, more violent than it's ever been before. Yet, based on unbiased information, the reality is it's the safest time to live on earth. Again, whatever you focus on programs your perception. I've included an interesting chart to prove my point.

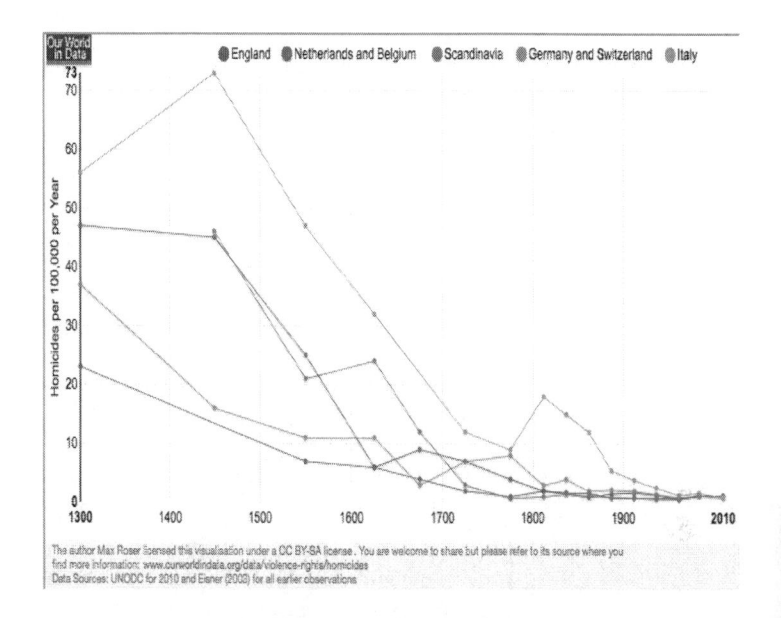

## Focus and Perception

My youngest child was hooked on Thomas the Tank Engine when he was young. He watched all the TV shows, and his older brother passed down his little diecast Thomas trains and tracks. He just loved Thomas. I'll never forget the following incident. He couldn't have been two years old, and we went to a restaurant, a Cracker Barrel where they have the country store. If you've visited Cracker Barrel stores, then you know those stores are just packed with merchandise. We weren't there two seconds before little Joey yells out, "Thomas!" We were looking and he's pointing up towards the corner, across the store. We ask him, "What do you mean Thomas? Thomas what?" He says, "Thomas the Tank Engine!" My wife and I were dumbfounded. What was he seeing? Well, we had to walk across the entire store and look closely—ten feet off the ground and on a stack of board games and puzzles, there was a tiny little two-inch Thomas the Tank Engine logo. You see, he had focused on it for so long that anything with that logo was the first thing he saw.

Do you spend your time focusing on unimportant things? If so, that's all you will see. Do you spend your energy, your talents, and your abilities for others? If you only spend time on yourself and invest your energy in yourself, you will become self-absorbed. What about your money? What would your credit statements accuse you of focusing on? Now, don't answer that out loud. However, where we spend our time, talent, and treasure, programs our filter and create our perception.

### Happiness and Perception

The former owner of the NFL franchise, the Seattle Seahawks, experienced four stages in his life. He was generally miserable, and created a belief that more stuff would make him happier. He worked hard in business, was successful, and purchased all kinds of stuff. However, he was still miserable. He called the first stage "stuff."

Then he went to stage two. He said, "I just need better stuff. The stuff I have isn't really the high-end stuff. I need the really high-end stuff." He made even more money, and he pursued his happiness through buying more stuff and better stuff. He purchased better homes, better cars, better airplanes, but he was still miserable.

He came to stage three and he thought, "You know what, it's got to be different stuff that makes you happy." So, he began pursuing things that nobody else had. He bought into an NFL franchise, the *Seattle Seahawks*, which was one of the most miserable times of his life.

Then a friend of his asked him to help on a trip. They were on a business trip, and he said, "Hey, we're going to stop in Bosnia, and we're going to give away about 75 wheelchairs to little kids who had their legs injured from landmines and things like that. I just need some help. We'll just make a quick stop." So, he went along with it. What's interesting is what happened while he was giving away a wheelchair to a 12-year-old boy. When he put the boy in the wheelchair and tried to roll him away, the boy started yelling. Through the interpreter he was saying, "Don't leave, don't leave, don't leave; you can't leave!" He said, "Ask the little boy why can't I leave?" The little boy looked at him and said, "I have to memorize your face because when I see you in heaven, I have to thank you one more time." That experience completely changed the man's life. At that moment, pure joy entered in. He had never experienced anything like that. Today, he has given away tens of thousands of wheelchairs, and it's a source of great happiness and joy for him.

## Mental Rehearsal and Perception

Major James Nesmith, a prisoner of war in North Vietnam was placed into a cage about five feet by four feet. He was not allowed any human contact. He was not let out of the cage. He was barely given enough food and water to survive. He nearly went insane. What he started doing was focusing on something different. Had he focused on his surroundings, his environment, he would have probably given up his will to live. He started playing golf in his mind, 18 holes a day at his favorite golf course. James was not a great golfer, but he loved to play. So, every day he determined to experience all the positive emotions and joys he got from playing a round of golf. He did that for nine years—nine years he played golf in his mind while a prisoner of war. I know you're in the tough spot. I know your life has challenges. But imagine being in a four feet by five feet cage in North Vietnam everyday of your life, yet somehow managing to maintain your sanity, and actually experiencing peace. When Major Nesmith was eventually rescued, one of the by-products, by the way, once he physically recouped, was he went on to play golf for real in the United States. His handicapped had improved to 23 strokes after having not touched a golf club in almost 10 years.

Mental rehearsal is more important than physical rehearsal. Some of you are rehearsing panic and fear, and you're getting really good at it. Others of you have rehearsed peace and overcoming, and you're getting really good at that.

Since your reticular system is the bouncer at the door to your mind, it's going to reject and accept information. What you need to do is get your bouncer to let in what you want in. What do you want to let in? You have to convince your bouncer to let it in because what you experience affects how you feel in any event. What would help you during a loss? What would you like to see in failure?

The brain is largely image driven. Decades ago, psychologists believed that you could store memories like books on a shelf. When you wanted to remember a certain memory, you would go, find that book, and you would look at the images.

Even though the brain is highly image driven, the reality is you don't remember anything; you imagine it. As a child maybe you were told to stop daydreaming, to stop imagining. However, that's the worst thing to do because your brain is imagination driven. Imagination is pre-living your future. James Nesmith imagined playing golf (with great skill) and he not only experienced the joy of playing, he improved his actual golf score. Worry is using your imagination for the worst possible outcome; it's programming your behavior for catastrophic results.

Your imagination is one of the gateways into your subconscious. Now lest you think you are the source of all creativity, and you are all-powerful and all knowing, I want to remind you that you have inspiration or ideas that come from somewhere else. If you've been given a dream, if you have an imagination, if you have something in your mind that means it is possible. Thomas Edison was asked after hundreds of failed experiments why he kept trying to pursue creating this thing called the light bulb. The critics told him, "It's impossible; you've failed hundreds of times. He said, "You don't understand how our brain works." Then Edison went on to explain, "I am not all powerful. This inspiration, which literally means to breathe into, was given to me, and I know if I can imagine it, it's possible." After hundreds of failed experiments, he got it right; he created the light bulb and changed the world.

## The Three T's: Time, Talent, Treasure

### Time

Spend some time and imagine a new perspective. One of the great disciplines is the discipline of abstinence. If you want to change your perspective, take away something. Shut off your TV for 90 days. Abstain from eating for 48 hours. Fasting is a great discipline. You know what? If you fast for two days, you will begin to see things differently. Many people go on a mission trip, and it changes their perspective, their paradigm, and their filter. Suddenly, their one-bedroom apartment is like a luxurious home because they realized that 80% of the world lives without running water.

Take time and visualize. Some people say they visualize, and some people say they don't visualize. The reality is everybody visualizes. Some people just choose to visualize success. You have two types of visualizations: anastrophic and catastrophic. Anastrophic visualization programs your mind to believe the world is conspiring to do good things to you. It believes that all things work together for your good. Catastrophic visualization programs your mind to believe the world is conspiring to do bad things to you. It believes all things work together for your demise. Remember, what you program yourself to focus on is what you'll experience.

Again, you're the average of the people you spend the most time with. Keep these three relationships in your life.

1. Have a mentor. A mentor is someone who has done what you want to do. I don't need someone who's always been fit

telling me how to lose weight because they've never done it. I want someone who was overweight for 20 years and then lost the weight. That's a good mentor. I don't need someone who was born rich telling me how to get out of debt. I need someone who was bankrupt. I need someone who lived in poverty, was upside down in their income and then figured it out. That's a mentor. Find that somebody who's done what you want to do. What response did they have to create the outcomes they got?

2. Have a friend who's in it with you. Someone who is in the boat with you because you can support each other and empathize and understand each other's struggles. Be careful that you don't have the kinds of friends who let you stay stuck and have no one leading and directing the boat.

3. Have a trainee, someone who needs your help. What have you done well? What have you accomplished? Find someone who wants to accomplish those things and help them. Did you know helping and training people reinforces your own self-worth, and self-esteem? It builds character, and it reinforces information to you. Depending on your learning style, you're going to retain a very small amount of what you read, and a very large amount of what you discuss or teach someone else. So, be teaching and training as you're learning this. If seven out of eight of your friends are broke, negative, overweight, angry, you're about to be eighth.

Create cognitive dissonance for your relationships. Again, you're going to use the 30-90-day principle to lock it in. And if you break the cycle, you'll go back to zero.

## Talent

What about your talent? Is it hard to find someone with less than you? Is it hard to find someone with a need? If you live in the United States, it's not hard at all. Find someone who has a need and meet their need. This is one of the sources of perpetual joy. Use the discipline of engagement, which is great for attitude issues. So, if you feel ungrateful, if you feel depressed, then commit to go to serve at a soup kitchen. Commit to go to the city mission. Commit to go on a mission trip. Commit one event this week, which is oriented on someone else's needs. It's not hard to find a need. Just go do it.

## Treasure

Create a vision board. Every success book I've ever read has some form of a vision board. A vision board is a board of images that are tied to what you want if your life worked out perfectly. Five years from now, if everything went perfect, what would your life look like? Where would you work? How much money would you have? What kind of relationships would you have? What kind of vacations would you take? What kind of skills would you acquire in five years? So, you create images. Some people like to get magazines, cut out pictures, and put them on a bulletin board. I have another suggestion. You look at your cellphone 500 to 1,000 times a day, so why not create a vision board using a picture app and then set it as your lock screen and home screen on your phone and computer so that 1,000 times a day you see your vision!

For some of you, before you can create a vision board, you may need to start by identifying and writing down your goals. Goal setting to me is imagining if everything went perfectly in your life, determining where you would be in, say, a year or five years or ten years. Then, use this as a starter and fill in the blank: As that imaginary person who (write down what it is that you want to do) what did I do to (write down what you did to do that). Take a look at this example to see how it works. If one of my goals is to take a Caribbean cruise, I would imagine that I've already accomplished it and then ask my imaginary self the following questions. The process would look like this:

- Question to myself: *"As that imaginary person who <u>took a Caribbean cruise</u>, what did you do to <u>take the cruise</u>?"*
  Answer: "Well, I saved."

- Question: "How much did you save?"
  Answer: $3,000.

- Question: "How did you save it? "
  Answer: "By putting away $280 every month for 11 months. I put it in the special vacation fund and didn't touch it."

Once you answer the questions, you go backwards, and you will have all the steps to go forward. I believe all the answers are inside your brain. You just have to get them out.

Take a seminar, or a personal development course. You know, only 5% of the world will willingly spend their own money on a seminar or on personal development. The other 95% expect someone else to do it for them. Put yourself in the top 5%!

By the way, 5% of the world owns 90% of the wealth. So, if you want to be in that 5%, do what 90% won't do. Form a healthy eating habit and exercise program. Move your body. Here are some ideas:

- Do the 21-day Fix program

- Do the P90X program

- Join a spin class

- Join a yoga class

Mind, body, and spirit are the key to health and happiness. If one is sick, the other two will be affected also.

## Questions

- If tomorrow you receive only what you've been thankful for today, what would you get?

- If tomorrow you receive only what you've been focusing on, what would you get?

- Where do you invest your most precious gift, your time?

- What would you have to focus on to see, feel, hear and experience what you want?

# Stress to Success Action Steps

*Commit to at least one action item from Time, Talent, and Treasure before you move on to the next chapter! Make it stick!*

Time:




Talent:




Treasure:

CHAPTER THREE

# Interpretation

*"All things are subject to interpretation. Whichever interpretation prevails at a given time is a function of power and not truth".* Friedrich Nietzsche

*"We cannot solve today's problems with the same kind of thinking that created them."* Albert Einstein

The third part of the human behavior model is interpretation. There are many things that can influence how you interpret events, but there are three basic interpretations of events:

1. We can interpret them as good, which would create positive emotions.
2. We can interpret them as bad and in turn create negative emotions.
3. We can interpret them as indifferent which will evoke no emotional response.

I heard a story about parents who had two children: a boy and a girl. The boy was always pessimistic, and the girl was always optimistic. The parents decided that they would play a trick on the children. It was Christmas time and their tradition was to buy presents for each child. They decided to get their pessimistic son anything he could ever dream of—all the latest video games, every expensive toy—the best of the best. They decided they would get their optimistic daughter a box filled with manure . . . yes, horse crap! Christmas came, and they waited to see the children's reactions. The boy opened his presents one by one. When he opened the first one, he said, "Oh, this game's already outdated." He opened another expensive toy and said, "Oh, yeah, these break though, and when you break them, they're expensive to replace." No matter how nice the gift was his reaction was negative. They went over to check on the daughter—the optimist—and she was inside the box throwing horse crap in the air. They asked her, "What are you doing?" She yelled from inside the box, "I know there's a pony in here; I just have to find it."

How do you interpret past events in your life? What rules do you make about current events? The reality is before you ever felt good, bad, or indifferent about a situation, you interpreted it. Interpretations are like the rules we make about life.

## Interpreting Events

### Interpreting Money

If you won the Power Ball Lottery for $300 million, how would you interpret that? Would you agree that most people would interpret that as good? The reality is this: five out of six super lottery winners end up ruining their lives. They ruin their relationships, their health, and their finances—in other words, 70% to 80% of all super lottery winners end up broke within seven years. Even worse, several winners have died tragically or witnessed those close to them suffer. One of those unlucky lottery winners was Abraham Shakespeare. Just weeks before he was killed, he told his mother he wished he had never won the lottery. Another one, Mr. Edwards, a former drug addict and a felon, won a $27 million jackpot in 2001 while unemployed in South Florida. He quickly blew through the money by purchasing a $1.6 million house in Palm Beach Gardens, three race horses, a fiber optics company, a Learjet, a limo business, a $200,000 Lamborghini Diablo and a multitude of other luxuries. Edwards and his wife returned to drug use and had numerous run-ins with police for possession of crack cocaine, pills, and heroin. He lost all of his money in just a few short years and ended up living in a storage unit surrounded by human feces.

But you told yourself winning this lottery is good, and how did you feel? You felt great. Even though the reality is, 70% to 80% of the time, you're going to ruin your life. So, let's not give events too much power. Events don't create your feelings. How you perceive events and then how you interpret what you perceive create all of your emotions.

Money does not make you happy. You could have an interpretation that money makes you happy, but the fact is money doesn't make you into anything that you weren't already. Money amplifies what's there. It reveals who you are. I've heard people say things like, "Oh, no, Dan, money changes people." My response is this: you can create that interpretation, albeit not factual, and it will affect how you feel. "Oh, no, Dan, my wife left me once she got money." I have news for you. Your wife left you emotionally a long time ago; she now has the means to carry it out and support herself. She left you emotionally, and she left you spiritually a long time ago. People also say things like, "Oh, no, such and such . . . he became selfish once he got money." Listen, he was selfish before. He just has more money to be selfish with.

Money does not make you happy. Money reveals what you are. "Oh, no, Dan, the Bible says, the love of money is the source of all evil." Well, that's not what the Bible says! The Bible says the love of money is the source of all sorts of evil. Money is not the root of all evil. The love of money is the root of all kinds of evil. Money is just money. Money gives you access and many times it reveals what's really there. Economists say 5% of the world's population owns almost 100% of the wealth. If you re-distributed it to everyone evenly, it's been said that within five to ten years, it would all be back in the hands of the same five percent.

How do you interpret events? Is money going to make you happy? Remember the owner of the *Seattle Seahawks* from chapter two? He had three interpretations of what he needed to be happy: stuff, better stuff, and different stuff. Then he finally realized that miserable starts with miser. One of the pillars of happiness is contributing to others.

## Interpretations Reframe Past Events

Remember our discussion about the model, E+R=O (Event plus Response equals Outcome)? We learned from the model that we cannot change past events. It's true that you cannot change the event, but you can reframe it. Reframing is a technique used by psychologists to change the way a past event is interpreted.

For example, years ago I would have said, "I dropped out of my honor classes because I really didn't have the guidance I needed from my parents because they were divorced. And since my mom was a single parent, she had to work more than she would have had to work if she and Dad remained married. She struggled to put herself through college, which took her away from me and being able to provide the guidance I needed." Or, I could say, "Boy, am I glad my parents were divorced because I didn't grow up in a household where my parents hated each other. Boy, am I glad I didn't go to college right out of high school, because with my low self-esteem and my low self-image, I probably would have done anything to get approval and gotten into all kinds of drugs and other destructive things." I could say, "Boy, am I glad I suffered for two years with clinical depression because it forced me to learn the truth about psychology, life, health, and happiness."

Some people interpret everything as negative. I know people, who if you gave them a donut, they would complain about the hole! Well, that's a choice to interpret the event as negative. Again, we have three choices regarding interpretations: good, bad, or different.

I heard a story about Victor, the dunce. Victor was told by his parents and by his guidance counselor, that he was a great guy. He was just not smart, and they encouraged him to drop out of high school. So, he did. They said, "You're going to be a laborer, and that's just the way it is because you're not smart, but you're a great guy." So, he became an itinerant worker, taking odd jobs. When they would run out of work, he would run out of a job, and so he would go get another job. He would even apply and say, "Hey, do you need any help?" And they'd say, "Well, we don't need much help." But he'd say, "Well, that's good because I'm not a lot of help, but I'm willing." He would do anything to support himself and make some money.

At one point, he had to take a test through a company that paid people to take assessments. He asked, "Do I have to be smart to take this assessment?" The company representative said, "Well, you don't have to; you could set the curve at the bottom." He said, "Okay. I'm not smart, but I'm willing to take the test if you'll pay me." The representative replied, "We'll pay you." He said, "Great." He did his best on the assessment and when he finished, he turned it in, and the rep had a funny look on his face. He said, "Something's not right," and Victor said, "What? You've never seen a score this low?"

So the company representative asked Victor to take the test again. Victor said, "Will you pay me again?" He wasn't that dumb. The rep said, "Sure, we'll pay you again." He took it the second time, and he focused and tried as hard as he could. Once again, he turned it in and the rep looked puzzled.

By now, Victor's self-esteem was hitting bottom, and he said, "Listen. I told you I wasn't smart." The representative replied, "Well, we'll pay you again. Will you take it one more time? However, we want the person who wrote the test to administer it." He said, "Listen, I'll do it one more time, but after that I'm done. I don't care if you pay me or not."

He took the test the third time. The person who wrote the test administered it, and he said, "Victor, you're a genius. This is an IQ evaluation test. You're smarter than me." Victor said, "That's impossible." The test administrator said, "I don't care what your parents told you. I don't care what your guidance counselor told you. You have an IQ over 160."

Victor's interpretation of the past changed after being told he was smart. Why did he struggle in school? Before he found out that he was a genius, his interpretation of failure was because he was dumb; now he realized he struggled in school because he was smarter than his teachers. Victor's intelligence level was always there. His interpretation of life changed that day. That morning, Victor woke up a dunce, and that night Victor went to bed a genius. He went on to create a six-figure income; he has several patents in his name and is the former chairman of the Mensa Society.

How do you interpret events like getting fired? One person gets fired and they get depressed and their depression turns into drinking and it ruins their life. Another person gets fired and says, "It's the best thing that ever happened to me. When one door closes a window opens." One of my interpretations is, all things work together for my good. Someone else's interpretation may be are all things work together for their bad.

I mentioned Thomas Edison earlier who had hundreds and hundreds of failed attempts at inventing the light bulb. In essence, Thomas Edison would say, "You don't understand failure. If you stop, that's when failure wins. Every failure leads me closer to the solution. Why would I stop now? I've eliminated hundreds and hundreds of ways not to do it. I am one step closer to the realization of my dream."

Failure is an event; it's not a person. The only time failure becomes a person is when you quit. When failure results in your quitting, that's the only time failure wins. Other than that it's really temporary resistance that develops the muscle to accomplish your destiny.

## Resistance Training Builds Muscle

It would probably be nearly impossible—if not impossible—for you to try to lift 250 pounds; right? Even if I encouraged you to use all of your will power, it would still be a difficult feat. And that's the problem that people experience when trying to accomplish a goal—they try to accomplish it using will power alone! Now, back to that 250 lb. weight, if you use too much will power, you can harm yourself and others. It's easier to start by using a small amount of resistance: 50 pounds, 75 pounds, and repeat the discipline of lifting what you can every day. Now, that discipline repeated over time will move you towards accomplishing what you wanted, lifting the 250 lb. weight. Failure is not permanent unless you quit your disciplines. You want to focus on the process not the event, and remember that every self-made success has failed multiple times. Consider these examples:

- Abraham Lincoln: His fiancé died. He failed in business twice. He had a nervous breakdown, and he was defeated in eight elections. Would you call him a failure? If you were defeated in eight elections, would you have tried the ninth time? Or would you have quit after one failed election? Would you have checked out when your fiancé died?

- Lucile Ball: She was told she was too shy and to just put her best food forward. Would you call her a failure?

- The Beatles were turned down by Decca Records who said, "Guitar groups are on the way out" and "The Beatles have no future in show business." Would you call The Beatles a failure?

- Jack Canfield, one of the authors of the Chicken Soup for the Soul series had 144 rejection letters from publishers. After 144 rejections the book was finally published and 500 million copies later it changed the world—it changed his life. When would you have quit . . . after 10 rejections, 20, 27, 40, 110?

- Walt Disney was fired from the Kansas City Star because his editor felt he lacked imagination, and he had no good ideas.

- Oprah Winfrey was publicly fired from her first TV job as an anchor in Baltimore for getting "too emotionally invested" in her stories.

- Steven Spielberg was rejected by the University of Southern California, School of Cinema Arts multiple times.

- In one of Fred Astaire's first screen test an executive wrote, "Can't act; slightly bald; can dance a little." Would you call Fred Astaire a failure?

- Vera Wang failed to make the 1968 U.S. Olympic Figure Skating team. She then became an editor at Vogue, but was passed over for the editor-in-chief position.

- Theodor Seuss Geisel, better known as Dr. Seuss, had his first book rejected by 27 different publishers. Failure?

- R.H. Macy had a series of failed retail ventures throughout his early career before he finally launched R.H. Macy and Company known today as Macy's.

When would you have quit? Now, the challenge is when you identify a goal and a purpose (later in chapter seven) you have to be 100% committed to not quitting. 98% commitment is a nightmare. If 98% of the airplanes land safely in Chicago O'Hare Airport every day, then two planes will crash every day because 98% is not enough. If my wife were faithful to me 98% of the time, that would be a nightmare because 98 or 99% commitment is no good. It's all or nothing. The world does not need people who are partially committed. It needs people that are committed to something 100%. That's what integrity is.

### If Only You Knew the End

Imagine you could write the end of your story. If you could create the last chapter of your life, what would it look like? Take a moment and think about that. What would you have accomplished? Who would you value? What difference in others would you have made? Once you know the ending, it should change how you interpret all events.

It's like watching a sporting event on DVR (back in my day it was videotape). You know, being from Cleveland, Ohio sports weren't always a real positive thing to watch! It wasn't creating positive emotions in my life.

Just last year our beloved Cleveland Cavaliers won the NBA finals championship. Now, imagine you didn't watch game seven live. You know the background. It was a seven games series, and we were down 3 to 1 facing elimination. We tied it up 3 to 3, so it was going to game seven. Game seven was back and forth, non-stop, ups and then downs, including over 20 lead changes. So let's imagine you didn't watch the game live. And some of you would say, "Wow, a game like that is so stressful. The game makes me worry. The game makes me stressed." That's actually not true. The fact that you don't know the ending makes you stressed.

Imagine you DVR the game because you were at work, and you couldn't watch it live. You don't know the score, and then you start to watch it—even on tape delay it would still be emotional because you don't know the ending. However, what if you fast-forward to the end and see that with 20 seconds left, your team hit a three pointer. Then fast-forward to watch the last six seconds and see that your team won. So, you would say, "Wow, we won. That's great." Now, what if you backed up and watched the game? Wouldn't all the fear and emotion go away? It's not the events that create your emotions. It's the fact that you're not sure what the end looks like.

## The Three T's: Time, Talent, Treasure

### Time

Choose an *outcome* you want in life. Write down the R (response/s) that creates the outcome you want. So, E plus R equals O.

- Pre-choose your interpretation or your response. Is getting fired good, bad or indifferent?

Here are some basic guidelines:

- What would be a response that creates the outcome you want when someone insults you?

- What would be a response that creates the outcome when you experience rejection?

- What would be a response that creates the outcome when you get hurt?

- Ask how could this work out for your good?

- What would have to be true for you to accept this and feel good?

- Ask yourself if your answer, based on interpretation, is accurate?

## Talent

- Ask how can this be used to benefit someone else?

- How could your temporary setback or resistance training help someone else?

- What gifts or abilities do you have as a result of the failures or pain in your life?

- Who could benefit from your story?

Become an inverse paranoid. An inverse paranoid says the world is out to get me for good.

## Treasure

In the Stephen Covey classic, *7 Habits of Highly Effective People*, he talks about a professor who took a pickle jar and put four or five large rocks in the pickle jar and asks his class "Is it full?" They said, "Yes." Then he took some pebbles, dropped them between the cracks, and said, "Is it full now?" They said, "It's really full now." Then he took some sand, and he sifted it into the spaces. See, the jar represents your life. We all get 24 hours a day. Some people seem to accomplish a lot more in the same amount of time. The big rocks are what really matters. The pebbles are things you just have to deal with. And, the sands, well, it's the stuff that doesn't really matter; it's stuff you cannot influence and don't really care about anyway. The rule is if you put the sand in the jar first and then the pebbles, the big rocks don't fit. If you put the big rocks in first, you'll even have time for social media or television. So, the question is, "What are your big rocks?"

Let me help you discover your most important tasks. Imagine, tomorrow you go to a funeral of a person you least want to see deceased. Maybe it's your child, maybe it's your spouse or sibling. You're on the way to that funeral. Ask yourself this question at that moment. "What matters to me today while I'm driving to that funeral?" However you answer that question—those are your big rocks. Put them in the jar first, prioritize those things.

Yes, we all have to do laundry and dishes and go to work and pay taxes. Those are the pebbles. However, if you don't prioritize, life will go by and the big rocks won't fit. Don't climb up the ladder of success and find out it was leaning against the wrong building.

Have a funeral day perspective. Make your decisions. Schedule your time and invest your time, talent and treasure based on that funeral day perspective. Right now take a moment and write down what would really matter to you on that day.

Commit to invest a percentage of your income to others and to your personal growth. This will convince your unconscious brain that you are serious.

## Questions

- How do you interpret events? Good, bad, or indifferent.

- How could your past failures help you succeed in the future?

- Has anyone ever experienced similar events and come out better for it?

# Stress to Success Action Steps

*Commit to at least one action item from Time, Talent, and Treasure before you move on to the next chapter! Make it stick!*

Time:




Talent:




Treasure:

CHAPTER FOUR

# Emotion

"*It may take me a long time to lose my temper, but once lost I could not find it with a dog.*" Mark Twain

"*The only thing to fear is fear itself.*" Franklin D. Roosevelt

"*Darkness cannot drive out darkness; only light can do that. Hate cannot drive out hate; only love can do that.*"
Dr. Martin Luther King

It's time to talk about emotion. Once again, in the human behavior model, when an event happens, you do not experience emotion first. First, you have a perception of the event, then, you interpret it: good, bad, or indifferent. And that interpretation then drives emotions.

When we experience emotions, we have two choices: we can express or suppress. Remember what suppression does? Suppression turns into depression which turns into disease which turns into disintegration. Many of us grew up hearing things like, "Suck it up. Be a man." Maybe you were nine years old when you heard that and thought to yourself, "Suck it up? I'm nine years old. I'm not supposed to feel emotion?"

One of the worst things you could tell someone is to bury their feelings. It's not always appropriate to express your emotions in the moment, so you learn to bracket for later expression. But again, you either want to resolve them or express them—not suppress them—because you don't want to go into an automatic depression which then leads to disease and disintegration of your emotional life, physical life, and spiritual life.

The rule with whatever emotion you may be feeling is this: no one outside of you is creating it. No one is making you feel anything. You're creating the emotion. Your brain is doing it. So, again, no blaming anyone or anything for how you feel. I'll accept that you may not be aware you're creating your emotions—whether it's conscious or unconscious—and that it's your brain doing it. For example, one person has an experience like ending a relationship and feels great. Another person ends a relationship and feels afraid. It's not the event. It's your perception and interpretation that drive your emotions. Once again, it's your brain; take 100% responsibility for it.

## Productive and Unproductive Emotions

There are two types of emotions: productive and unproductive. Productive emotions create outcomes that produce more health and happiness. Unproductive emotions create outcomes that reduce our health and happiness.

### Sources of Emotion

What are the sources of emotion? If you took all the different kinds of emotions that you have felt or could possibly feel, and you trace them all the way back to their sources, what you're going to find is that you have two sources of all emotions. The first source is love.

## Productive Emotions

Love is the source of all productive emotions. Now, by productive emotions, I mean if you repeated this emotion over and over and over, and you held this emotion daily, it would be productive. In other words, it would cause you to grow physically, mentally, and spiritually. It would increase your health. It would cause you to operate in a highly productive manner.

Love-based emotions are productive. What are some love-based emotions? The most powerful emotion for changing your vibrational energy, your psychology, and the way you feel, is gratitude.

Gratitude changes your energy metaphysically. Gratitude activates parts of your brain that otherwise lie dormant. So, gratitude is a love-based emotion. Remember, cognitive dissonance? When you go on a mission trip, and realize that 80 percent of the people on earth live without things that you take for granted, you come back to your home and experience gratitude for what you have.

Faith is a love-based emotion. Faith is the substance of things hoped for. So, faith repeatedly creates positive and productive states of mind and health.

Joy for others and joy for yourself is a positive productive emotion.

## What about Anger?

Is anger productive or unproductive? It depends on its source. If it's sourced out of love then it's productive. Love-based anger will produce more character, and produce more health.

Dr. Martin Luther King was angry, but his anger was sourced out of love. Hitler was angry, but his anger was *not* sourced out of love. We will talk more about that later.

Other love-based emotions are serenity, peace, calm, curiosity, playfulness, contentment. So, on the one side of our brain we're sourcing emotions out of love. Love-based emotions are productive which means they lead to a manageable state of mind and health.

## Fear-based Emotions

What is the opposite of love? If some emotions are sourced out of love, what would be the opposite? Most people think of hate, but that's not necessarily true. The opposite of love-based or love-sourced emotions are fear-based emotions.

Fear-based emotions are unproductive. They lead to an unmanageable state. They decline your health, your emotions, and your spiritual life. Fear-based emotions do not produce life. What types of fear-based emotions do we have? Jealousy is a fear-based emotion; it's the fear of not being good enough.

Anger, again, can be sourced out of love or fear. Hitler had anger sourced out of fear: fear of different people, fear of losing power, fear of losing prestige.

Resentment is another powerful fear-based emotion; in fact, it is one of the most powerful fear-based emotions. To harbor resentment towards someone actually kills *you*. Resentment is like drinking poison every day and hoping the other person dies. So, unforgiveness and resentment are unproductive emotions. If you repeat these, they actually kill you.

There have been studies of the effects of gratitude and resentment on people's lives. Resentment leads to all kinds of negative states, and one of the negative physical states is it puts your body in an acidic mode. Your body has a pH level; it's either alkaline or acidic. If your body has 7.5 pH or higher, that's good; that's high alkaline. This is important because an alkaline environment neutralizes. What does it neutralize? It neutralizes all kinds of diseases, including cancer. An acidic environment actually feeds cancer and causes it to grow. So, resentment and unforgiveness are unproductive. If you repeatedly hold them, they can kill you, literally.

Guilt is an unproductive emotion. Panic is an unproductive emotion as is anxiety, negative stress, and even rushing. Did you know rushing was an emotion? Rushing is a fear of something bad happening if you're not on time.

## Fight or Flight

Unproductive emotions lead to an unmanageable state. When we experience an unproductive emotion through our perception and interpretation that something bad will happen, it can trigger what's called the *fight-or-flight syndrome*. It's also known as *fight-flight-or-freeze*. This is often called the *general adaptation syndrome* in Psychology books, and most people refer to it as fight-or-flight. There are some amazing things that happen when we go into fight-or-flight.

First of all, there is a perceived event that's negative and you interpret it as bad. Then, your brain goes into a self-defense mode. Before I explain everything that's happening mentally and physiologically, when you perceive a threat and go into fight-or-flight, I want to answer the question: why do we have this fight-or-flight syndrome?

When I asked this question all over the country, I get the same answer: It's a self-defense mechanism, and we're born with it. Now, I want to ask you something. Were you ever chased by a lion or a tiger through the jungle? Largely the answer is no. So, we do have a self-defense mechanism but what triggers the self-defense is always a learned response.

Let me give you an example. A two-year-old is not afraid to ask a question; however, many times a 32-year-old is afraid to ask a question. A two-year-old is not afraid to speak in public most of the time. A 22-year-old might be afraid and could go into this fight-or-flight response.

We learn what to interpret as bad. We learn through focus how to see threats. Asking, by the way, is one of the core skills you need to be successful in this life. You're going to get 100% of what you don't ask for you; you're going to get "No." If you don't ask, you have zero chances of getting it. So, ask, ask, ask! Most of us have developed a sub-conscious fear of asking.

Public speaking is ranked as the highest fear more than drowning or more than being eaten by sharks. People are more afraid of public speaking. Isn't that unbelievable? Yet, there's really nothing to be afraid of; it's a learned fear. Are we naturally afraid of public speaking? No!

So, do we have this self-defense mechanism in our brain? Yes. Is it that we're automatically born with this fear? No. You learn to be afraid of things. One child falls down and skins her knee and laughs it off. Another child falls down and bumps his knee and loses his mind. It was learned and reinforced.

So, what's happening? First, your brain perceives a threat that you interpret to be valid—whether it is or not, it doesn't matter. You think it is. Your brain is going to do some things to help you out because it wants to go into self-preservation mode. One of the things it does is it blocks the transmitters and receptors to the frontal cortex which means your brain, the logical part, is disconnected when you're emotional. You cannot think logically. You cannot communicate effectively.

Have you ever been in a situation where you were upset, and you just gave in on the argument because you couldn't think of the right answer? Then 20 minutes later you came up with three responses that would have won the argument? "Oh, I hate that. Why couldn't I think of that in the moment?" That easy...because your brain was disconnected! The cortex disconnects from your ears and from your mouth, which means you don't hear logic; therefore, you can't communicate logically.

Have you ever been emotional and blurted out something you didn't mean? Now, you're thinking, "Oh, my gosh. Now, I'm in bigger trouble. Why did I even say that?" Well, once again you can communicate, but it's not logical.

It's also one of the reasons why telling someone to calm down almost never calms the person down. Logic does not diffuse. Logic cannot enter or come out during the fight-or-flight syndrome. Your brain is going to give you two choices: you're going to get away from this threat, or you're going to fight it.

Not only are your mouth and ears disconnected, there are some physiological things that are happening as well. Your brain thinks you're going to die, so it's trying to protect you. It believes you're either going to run a half-marathon (which I think is 13.1 miles), or you're going to fight five rounds in the ultimate fighting championship. That's what you have convinced your brain is going to happen through your perceived and interpreted threat.

At this point, your brain is directing your body, telling it exactly what to do: "So, we have to get your heart rate up says your brain. If you haven't been doing your cardio, I've got you. We're going to increase your heart rate to get your muscles pumping, your blood pumping, and oxygen to the muscles." Your blood pressure rises. Glucose gets sent to your muscles. Now, your brain is thinking, "Wow! We need some quick energy right now." So it's going to produce sugar, glucose for quick energy.

Cortisol is released. Did you know you have a pharmacist in your brain? That pharmacist will trigger and release all kinds of chemicals, and drugs based on what it thinks you need. Well, you told your brain you were going to die; it believed you. Now, it's releasing cortisol.

One of the benefits of cortisol is that it makes you a little bit impervious to pain. It also makes you a little bit edgy. High spikes of cortisol can make you very irritable, which would be great if you were fighting five rounds in the UFC.

Did you know your digestion slows or stops during the general adaptation syndrome? I realized this truth looking back at when I was stressing myself out 20 to 30 times a day at work and at home. My brain decided to shut off my digestion. So, if I ate a whole meal or a sandwich, that food would just sit there in my stomach for days because my digestion had stopped.

Your muscles tense and you sweat during the general adaptation syndrome. Your brain believes you're going to die. You created that perception, consciously or unconsciously, because you interpreted it as bad. If that's true, then you can interpret it differently. You can change it. You're not being chased by tigers. You're not going to die. We learn what to be afraid of. I want to ask you right now if what you believe was negative, is it true? Is it true for everyone? Most of the time, it's largely subconscious.

My wife and I took our kids to a water park. Now, some of these indoor water parks are amazing. I mean, the slides are unbelievable. They are so tall. Some of them are very aggressive. There's this one slide that will basically remove or internalize your swimsuit if you're not careful because you have to keep your legs locked together. Unbelievable!

Well, this was not that water park. This was a knock-off generic water park. We had a coupon for some no name hotel/waterpark. It was winter in Ohio, which means you really can't go outside. When we got there, my wife and I were so disappointed. It had some decent slides, but it was nothing like we thought, but the kids were having a great time.

The slides come down two stories, and they take you through a little tunnel and then you land in a puddle. There are no pools in this water park. There are just some puddles. By that, I mean, little landing areas about a foot and a half deep with water. Once you get out of the puddle, you go, and you do the slide again and again.

Well, we were standing there watching the kids running around, making noise, and having a good time. We were bored, so we were just talking and trying to figure out why there was a life-guard since there was no pool. The lifeguard was this teenaged boy with perfect hair and a nice tan, but he was fully-clothed because he was guarding a puddle. Apparently, he did not expect to get wet!

Suddenly, we see a grown man come down one of the bigger slides for that park—but again not a very intense slide, by my standard. He comes out of the tunnel and hits the water and starts swimming for his life. He was face down, moving his arms and legs like he was in the Olympics. Michael Phelps would have nothing on this man. He started splashing and kicking, and immediately we laughed. What was he doing? The lifeguard eventually caught on that this man was in the general adaptation syndrome that is the fight/flight mode. You see, the man on the slide convinced himself that he was drowning. He was disoriented. His brain interpreted the water as "you are drowning."

Now, left to himself, that man would have drowned. Even early on, the lifeguard went over to the man and yelled, "Sir, stand up. Stand up. Sit up." The water was a foot and a half deep. But because the man's brain was completely disconnected, he was convinced that he was drowning. His brain was interpreting the water as verification of his fear that he would drown.

The poor lifeguard had to get in there and get his clothes wet and roll this man over at risk of his own danger because the man almost took his head off with his big arms swinging wildly. Eventually, he pulled the man out of the water. The man opened his eyes and when he became oriented to his surroundings you could see his heart just pounding through his chest. If he had been left alone his greatest fear would have come true, and he would have drowned. I'm willing to bet that on the way up the stairs to the slide, he kept saying to himself, "Don't worry. You won't drown. You won't drown. You won't drown. You won't drown." Well, here's the thing about psychology: it's more image-driven, than word-driven. So his brain didn't hear "won't drown." It heard the word "drown, drown, drown." He got down the slide, got disoriented, hit the water, and interpreted it as, "See, I told you, you are drowning," and his brain disconnected.

## Visualization

You are the center of all the movies in your brain. You are the center of all the images and imaginations of your brain. You experience the emotional and physiological sensations of those images or what I like to call movies. This is why romance novels are so successful and impactful because you experience the emotional equivalency as if it were you.

Well, here's what those in the personal development field know. Successful people watch movies in their head of past successes. The unconscious mind is so powerful; it doesn't know the difference between a real or perceived event. But when a successful person has a new opportunity, they look back at all the movies where they succeeded. "Oh, yes. Remember in high school? I won the debate. Remember, in college, I did this, or in my 20s, I did that?" And the brain chalks all those memories up as real events. Let's say you only had three successes in your life. If you replay those a thousand times, you will get the emotional equivalency as if they happened a thousand times.

Unhappy, unsuccessful people, who may have one or two past failures, play them over and over. Again, you are the center of your movie. So, even though that event only happened one or two times, or maybe it never happened at all, when you replay it as if it did, your brain says, "Oh, no. You can't do it. You're a failure. You're a loser."

Do you know someone that had something "bad" happened to them 20 years ago? Maybe a relationship failed, and all they do is talk about it, every day. Every time they do that, they reinforce a horse trail or neurological loop in their brain. The more loops you have the more automatic that feeling becomes.

Always imagine yourself operating in success for what you want. If you can't see yourself being successful, then that's your biggest issue. Your feelings are largely coming from those images. Have you ever watched one of those *YouTube* videos where skateboarders break their ankle or falls off of a ramp? Or sometimes these people who try to dive into the swimming pool and hit the edge of the pool, and you get a shock wave of pain down your spine from watching it? Well, that's your brain interpreting the images as if it's happening to you. Imagine the power you have to change how you feel. Visualization is pre-living what you want your body to experience. So, again, always create images that are for what you want.

The University of Chicago took three groups of basketball players and performed an experiment to see if they could improve their free throw shooting.

Group one was told to practice shooting free throws, 30 minutes a day for a month. That group improved about 24% overall.

Group two was told not to touch a basketball for a month, and they did not. They had no change, no improvement, but they didn't decline because they already had pretty good form, and they had been playing basketball for most of their lives.

Group three was told not to touch a basketball for a month, and for ten minutes a day to shut their eyes, get relaxed and shoot free throws in their minds. Further, every visualized free throw had to be perfect form and with a perfect swish.

What they found out is the group that did the visual practice experienced almost the same improvement doing ten minutes of visualization as the group that practiced for 30 minutes each day. The visualization group improved their free throw shooting 23%, a mere 1% less than the group that actually practiced.

Let me ask you a rhetorical question: what is easier, 30 minutes of practice or ten minutes of visualization? Now, for the best results, I suggest you combine both. You should practice, and make sure you can visualize yourself being successful.

Emotions are like a tabletop. A tabletop is typically made of wood or some other material. But, it's not a table with just the top; it needs legs. The legs are references given to the table so that it can stand. My point is if you have an emotion or perception of an emotion, it can't stand unless you reference negative past or positive past events. The more legs you have, the stronger that belief or that emotion becomes. You should always reference the emotion you want.

I'll give you an example. What if you decide that you can't speak in public because one time you tried it, and it didn't work? If you say it doesn't work 20 times—even though you only did it, and it didn't work that one-time—you will create a pretty strong emotional belief that you can't do it. Public speaking is a learnable skill, and because you have learned other things, you can learn public speaking. If you reinforce that over and over, it will support you feeling good about public speaking. It's not public speaking that makes you feel one way or the other. It's the images and the references you have about it, positive or negative.

Choose to reinforce the feelings that you want regarding relationships, falling in love, dating, being married, being single, whatever. It's not your circumstances that create your feelings. It's the images and the references you have. Remember the law of attraction? You're going to become what you think about most of the time. Your feelings, therefore, are an outcome of your subconscious program.

If a farmer has some fertile land, he can plant whatever he wants. On one row, he plants corn and on another row, he plants poison. He waters and takes care of the land; consequently, whatever he planted will grow—corn and poison. Now, remember, I'm comparing the land to the brain. The land doesn't care what's planted. It's going to yield whatever the farmer planted. It's not going to tell him what to plant. I know too many people who expect one thing when they have planted something else. You can't get tomatoes if all you planted were weeds!

I don't know if you have ever gardened in your backyard. But it would be ridiculous to expect zucchini if all you plant is corn, wouldn't it? But what if you planted for a year, and then you took the next year off and decided not to plant anything? Would anything grow? You know, if you create a garden and leave it sit dormant for one year, you will have weeds in there in no time, because weeds blow in from other people's yards.

In this analogy, the weeds are the negativity that's so pervasive in our culture. So, if you decide not to plant, you can assume that you're going to have a negative perception, a negative interpretation, and unproductive emotions about your life.

## The Three C's

When it comes to happiness, there are three pillars. I call them the three C's of what makes people really feel happy. The three C's are: contribution, community, and continuing education.

### Contribution

One of the sources of all happiness is when we contribute to other people. There are two seas in the Middle East: the Sea of Galilee and the Dead Sea. What's interesting is they're sourced from the same river. The Sea of Galilee is full of life. It has birds, fish, and all kinds of vegetation. The Dead Sea is exactly that . . . dead, nothing grows in it. How could two bodies of water that are sourced from the same thing produce such different results? The Sea of Galilee has an outlet that feeds other bodies of water, and the Dead Sea does not. All the water that flows into it just sits and becomes stagnant. That's how it works in your life.

## Miserable Starts with Miser

Many years ago, we had only one vehicle, and we had two children who had to be transported here and there. It was stressful. I was doing contracting work. I didn't have a vehicle, and I couldn't afford one. We were on public assistance. A family member came over with a vehicle and a title. He wanted to give me this vehicle, and I rejected it. I said, "I can't take this." I'll never forget his response. He said, "How could you be so selfish?" I said, "I'm selfish by not taking it?" He said, "Yes. You're going to rob me of the joy that I get for giving you this vehicle. That's selfish of you." I really didn't have an answer to that, so I reluctantly accepted it. I offered to pay him back over time since I didn't have the money then. He said, "No. I'm giving it to you." I never forgot how that felt.

About four or five years ago we were in a much better financial state. We had a van, and we finally paid it off. It was a Toyota van, and they're famous for running forever. I thought, "We are never getting rid of this van, because it's paid for now. It's going to run another five or ten years at least. I don't want a new van. I don't want a van payment."

My wife came to me and said she felt impressed to give our van to a family we knew. I said, "Why?" She said, "Well, they have three kids now. They have a small car, and they do basketball outreach for inner-city kids. Every week they taxi teenagers to and from their weekly basketball." I had to admit that he was really investing in these kids. He would bring different speakers in at half-time, and they would speak about life and faith and other things. He would cram all these kids into his car, and they would get 75, 80, 90 kids a week. She said, "I think they need the van more than we do." I thought, "Well, I don't agree with that. I think we need the van because I don't want a van payment. We really don't have the money to buy a new van." But I thought back to when someone gave me a vehicle, and how much of a blessing it was for our family, so, I agreed.

We had the van detailed. We had things fixed on it like little handles that were slightly broken that we wouldn't have fixed for ourselves. The van had some miles on it, but it was in really great shape. We took the van to this family, along with the title, and said, "We just want to give you this van." They were so appreciative.

Everyone thinks the blessing is in the act of giving, but it's deeper than that. Let me tell you something. I saw that van just a couple of years ago. It's still running. It has to have over 200,000 miles on it. When I saw that van years later still going, still serving their needs, right now as I'm writing to you, I still experience joy. Contribution is one of the pillars of joy. Do something for someone else.

## Community

There is a human need that we want to be part of something bigger. Kids will join gangs to be part of a community. Even if it's a horrible community, we want to be on a team. We want a jersey. We want to be in the group. If you walked into a place and everyone was wearing a blue hat, and you were wearing a white hat, you would not feel connected; it would lower your feeling of significance. We want to be part of something. Join a community of people who share your values and beliefs. Become a part of something bigger.

One of the cores to happiness is to know people and be known. Who knows you and who do you know? Whose team are you on? What group are you in? It's sometimes called the transcending cause, which is something that's going to last longer than you. If you're not happy, I'm willing to bet (1) you're probably not contributing a lot to others, or (2) you're not part of a bigger group.

## Continuing Education

Continuing education does not necessarily mean attending college; it means never ending learning—continuous and never-ending improvement and learning.

Kids experience a ton of joy because they're always learning. I'll never forget when all of my kids learned to play that plastic recorder song flute and how excited they would get. I remember my youngest attended a school that had computers for the students, and they could record themselves accomplishing something. He would learn all kinds of things and every few weeks I would get a little video clip of him saying, "Hey, Dad, watch this!" For him, learning something new was joyous and exciting.

Adults, on the other hand, tend to stop the learning process after a certain point in our lives. We seem to think that we know all there is to know about our careers, our lives, and the world. Nothing could be further from the truth! Listen, the minute you stop growing your brain is the minute your happiness starts to diminish. So, learn something. Grow.

## Your Mind

Become aware of the images in your mind when you're upset, either positive or negative. Replace negative images with positive images. Re-record negative movies or past events with a funny twist as a way to take away their power. In a situation where maybe you felt intimated or embarrassed, find a way to replay the movie with a funny twist.

Earlier, I told you psychologists once thought we have the mental equivalent of books and bookshelves in our brains. The reality is there are no books and there are no bookshelves. When you go to remember an event, your brain walks this pathway and rewrites it as you go. Since you're rewriting, what if you just put a little twist on it, like it really wasn't embarrassment, it was just fun? It really wasn't bullying, it was just childish behavior. Every time you rewrite it, start to put less of a painful twist on it and more of a humorous twist on it.

I learned this technique from one of my favorite teachers, Anthony Robbins. He replays past painful events he experienced with others by imagining those people with Disney characters on their head. For example, he imagines his boss having Goofy's face and wearing Goofy's shoes. Then, he fast forwards and rewinds, and fast forwards and rewinds, to the point where it's ridiculous. He takes a negative past event, and he rewrites all the emotions to be more positive, more humorous, and less fearful. Try it!

## Gratitude

You should express gratitude first thing in the morning. What's great? What are you thankful for? Write it down. There's a ton of work done on writing down what you want. If you really want to lock it into your brain, write it down.

Write a love letter to someone else. Tell someone that you appreciate them, for example, co-workers, employees, family members, friends, the police department, recreation directors, coaches, and teachers. One of the top three reasons people quit their jobs in the United States is that they don't feel appreciated. So, there is no shortage of need out there for people who need to be appreciated. Just take five minutes every day and write one letter of appreciation to someone.

Learn other people's love languages. In Gary Chapman's book *The Five Love Languages* he talks about five ways people feel appreciation: acts of service, quality time, physical touch, words of affirmation, and gifts. Fill someone's love tank today. Make it a habit and watch your happiness go up.

## Body

Your physiology can back feed into your psychology. When your psychology is creating a fear response, you can use your physiology to change how you feel. One technique is called abdominal breathing or regulating your nervous system through proper breathing. In layman's terms, there is some hardware, if you will, behind your abdomen—the sympathetic and parasympathetic nervous system. If find yourself going into a fight-or-flight response, and you're starting to sweat and breathe heavy, etc., follow these four steps to change how you're feeling:

1. Breathe in for four seconds through your nose and fill up your abdomen. Your belly should get pushed out. I know it's not very sexy to do in public, but you're going to look like you have a pot belly for a second.
2. Hold that breath for four seconds. During those four seconds, you're going to confuse your brain because it's trying to increase your heart rate, and you're slowing it down.
3. Exhale for four seconds slowly like a leaking basketball; just slowly let all the air out until your abdomen pushes against that nerve.
4. Repeat two or three times.

I do a combination of abdominal breathing and a technique I learned from my military training. Military or police officers will sip ice-cold water slowly when they're getting nervous to shut off the fight-or-flight response. They can't have their brain disconnected while handling heavy artillery because they might engage in friendly fire and shoot their own people. So they'll sip cold water. Follow these steps to do the combination technique.

1. Breathe in for four seconds.
2. Hold it. Become aware of your thoughts, aware of your images; are they positive or negative?
3. Exhale, and then sip hot tea or ice cold water slowly.

4. Repeat steps 1–3. In the time it takes to sip a cup of tea, you can totally reverse the negative physiological effects.

## Television

Replace one hour of TV watching per day. You might say, "What can I do instead?" Well, if you're watching four to six hours a day, let's just take one hour, use 20 minutes to exercise every day, 20 minutes to read something informational, learn a language, whatever, and 20 minutes to meditate or pray each day.

## Move Your Body

The smaller the space you occupy, the more difficult it is to reverse negative energy. So, if you're depressed or fearful, take up space. Wave your arms up and down. Imagine you just finished a 5k. Jump up and down. Put your arms in the air like you're crossing a finish line. Take up space. Hold the power pose. Put your hands on your hips, stick out your chest for five minutes, and you can reverse negative physiology.

## Spiritual

Use visualization to reverse negative emotions. Pre-live events and change the ending. Start and end your day with positivity. There are great websites that will give you a dose of positivity first thing in the morning:

- simpletruths.com
- motivational minute

- ourdailybread.org.

## Forgiveness

Who do you have to forgive? As much as it's up to you, strive to be at peace with all people. Recall what I told you earlier about resentment—it's like drinking poison every day and hoping the other person will die. Resolve today to let resentment go and forgive the offender. It doesn't mean they have to come back and say they're sorry. It means as much as it's up to you, you forgive them, and you forgive yourself. Remember and write down all of the mercy and grace you are receiving every day.

# Stress to Success Action Steps

*Commit to working on Your Mind before you move on to the next chapter! Make it stick!*

Gratitude:

Body:

Forgiveness:

CHAPTER FIVE

# Behavior

*Your behavior reveals your beliefs whether you know it or not."*
Daniel Spacagna

*"Act as if what you do makes a difference, because it does."*
William James

Knowledge is not power. The most immediate cause of your outcomes—be they financial, emotional, relational, or vocational—is your behavior. Change your behavior and you change your outcomes.

With all the information available in the 21st century like *Google*, or *WebMD*, we should be free of all destructive behaviors. We know that eating right and exercise is important, yet the U.S. has the highest rate of obesity in the world. We understand early-childhood development is essential to raising positive and productive children, yet society has lost control of its youth. We know the stages of relationships and have books and seminars teaching us how to have healthy marriages, yet the divorce rate continues above 50%, even though less people are getting married today.

In Alan Deutschman's book, *Change or Die: The Three Keys to Change at Work and in Life*, he studied individuals who were given a negative diagnosis and told if they did not change their behavior, they would perish. It floored him when he found out that 90% of the people who were told, "Change your behavior or die," died. This prompted him to study why people do what they do and why even the threat of death wasn't enough to help people change. Deutschman said, "The reason people don't change is not that they cannot change. It is not that they didn't want to change. The reason is they did not understand change or have the right tools to affect change."

Why don't people change? Well, first of all, five-sixths of the brain is wired not to change. The unconscious part of your brain doesn't want to change. It believes same is safe. Most people will not retrain that part of their brain to get the behavior they want. There's a method that's commonly taught to train the unconscious, and it uses the acronym FIRE: Focus, Intensity, Repetition, Every Day. People spend more time focusing on things they don't want. They repeat songs and advertisements that have no bearing on their best life or their personal growth. They devote too much time in intense gossip and fear. Furthermore, they're not consistent. They'll do something one way for a day and then do five things a different way the next five days. Let's separate some myths from some facts to get a better understanding of change.

## Myths or Facts

Commonly I hear "change takes time." Have you heard that? That's a myth. Change happens in an instant. Convincing your brain, especially the unconscious part, to change can take some time—30, 90 days, six months, maybe even 40 years. We all know someone who chain-smoked for many years and tried different things to stop smoking. Then, something happened one day, and they just stopped. The change happened instantly. What took time was preparing themselves to change, and convincing their unconscious that they wanted to change.

When I came out of my clinical depression—two years of not being able to eat—change happened in one day. One day, I couldn't eat, and the next day I could. What I didn't realize is I had started pursuing truth, and I had started accidentally applying some of the steps that I'm sharing with you. Consequently, I experienced the change instantly one day. However, it was probably several weeks and maybe even months of programming in my unconscious to allow the change to happen. Several months later, I found myself being able to switch back and forth—if you remember the horse-and-rider analogy—to old patterns and new patterns. I've learned that even though you have a new pattern of behavior, the old path is always available. I want you to remember, old neurological loops are always there. You can choose consciously and unconsciously to stay on the right path.

"The older you are, the harder it is to change." Have you heard that? That is also a myth. Age has nothing to do with it. What you have done with your time has more to do with it than your age. I know young people whose brains are extremely inflexible. That's because they do the same thing every day for five or six years. I know older people who have very flexible brains and adapt quickly to changes. Again, age has nothing to do with it. The majority of people stop learning in their early 20s and then by the time they are 40, 50, or 60, they have a harder time adapting and breaking habits. However, it's not their age that presents the challenge; it's what they've done with their time that presents the challenge. If you took a horse and walked it around your backyard one time, it wouldn't damage the grass, would it? But what if you walked it around that exact same path for 25 years? Would grass grow where you walked that horse? No. That's an example of what age does. It's not really the age. It's the fact that we always engage in the same pattern of behavior all the time, and that pattern reinforces the behavior.

Mitchell Baker once said, "Change is uncomfortable." That statement is a fact; that's not a myth. Change is uncomfortable. Your unconscious brain always fights for the old pathways. It rejects change until you convince it that the change is good for you.

If you've been in one of my seminars, you've probably done this change exercise before. If not, I'm sure you'll be amazed at the results. Fold your hands together; interlock your fingers and your thumbs. Now, notice which thumb is on top; is it your right thumb or your left thumb? There's no right or wrong way to do this because there's no moral, ethical, or religious reason to fold your hands, one way or the other, that I'm aware of. However, your brain does have a preference. What I'd like you to do now is just switch; interlock your fingers the opposite way. So, if your right thumb is on top, put your left thumb on top; if your left thumb is on top, put your right thumb on top. How does that feel? It feels uncomfortable, doesn't it? Now, I want you to hold that position and be uncomfortable for just a minute while I explain what's going on in your unconscious.

There are three things that your unconscious is telling you—your horse, if you will.

1. "This is wrong."
2. "This is dangerous"
3. "Go back."

This is the exact cycle we all experience when faced with change. Your unconscious tells you the change is wrong. It tells you that you shouldn't be doing it that way because that way is dangerous. It tells you if you keep it up, you're going to get injured, and there will be negative effects. Then it screams to you to go back! It wants you to go back to the job you hate, and to go back to the behavior that created the horrible outcome. Go back to the abusive relationship. Go back to spending more than you make. It pushes you back into the old patterns. If you haven't already, switch your hands back into what feels normal for you. How does that feel; it feels much better, right? Let me give the same warning I give my seminar and conference participants: If you're not willing to be uncomfortable for a short season you will not change, or you'll have a very difficult time changing!

Another myth is, "You have to want to change." Even if you don't want to change, you will change if you apply the principles. Remember that luxury car you test drove? You don't want a new car. However, if you keep hanging out in luxury cars, or you keep borrowing your friend's BMW or Lexus, eventually your car will not feel comfortable. You will move towards that newer, luxury car.

Back in my teens, and early 20s, I was offered to join a band for pay. It was the first time I was paid to play music. As a young musician, I thought it was cool someone wanted to pay me to play music. The problem was it was a country band, and I didn't listen to country music. I did not want to listen to country music nor did I even like country music. I accepted the offer which happened to coincide with Garth Brooks' emergence onto the country music scene. I remember one of our early gigs. I wore a cowboy hat, and I looked like a cowboy. Someone from the establishment came up to me and said, "You know, you look a little like Garth Brooks." I said, "Who?" He just burst out laughing. I had no idea who Garth Brooks was. The interesting thing is even though I didn't want to like country music there were some songs that just stuck with me. Frankly, I still don't choose country music, but if I hear "Shameless" by Garth Brooks, it takes me right back, and I get a positive emotional experience from it. I like certain country songs now. My point is, you don't have to want to change. If you stick to the disciplines, if you train your unconscious, you will change.

John Heywood has been credited with the quote, "You can lead a horse to water, but you can't make him drink." In other words, you cannot make someone else change. Is that a fact or myth? That's a fact. You cannot control someone else's brain, but you can influence their behavior. Think of it like this, you cannot make a horse drink, but you could feed it salt, and it would get thirsty.

Rather than focus on trying to change other people, I recommend you focus on changing yourself. I realize, though, it can be difficult trying to figure out what you should or should not focus on. My *Lay Your Cards on the Table* exercise will help you. You'll need a pen or marker, a pack of *Post-It* notes, and a table.

- Write down one concern per *Post-It* note. For example, your health, your wealth, your family, your relationships, world peace, the economy, the weather, etc.
- Place those concerns that you can influence on the left-upper side of the table.
- Take a look at what you placed on the left-upper side and determine which of these do you have absolute—and I do mean absolute—control over and move them to the lower-right side.

Are the concerns on the left-upper side of the table representative of your belief that you really can influence them? Can you influence your kids, or your co-workers or your health or your wealth? What about the items you moved to the lower-right side? How many do you really have absolute control over? I submit that you cannot control your spouse. You cannot control your kids. I hope you can see through this demonstration that your response is the only thing you can control.

You want to focus on controlling yourself and influencing what you can and not worrying about the rest. That fact is, you cannot make someone change. However, with the right amount of skill, you can influence them and create cognitive dissonance causing them to do one of three things:

1. Stop hanging around you
2. Change
3. Try to get you to change back

Keep this in mind the next time you're trying to change someone else!

One of the biggest challenges with behavior is that people identify certain behaviors as rude. I teach classes on dealing with difficult people, and this is one of my favorite points to make: there is no such behavior as rude. Rude is a perception.

Let me give you an example. My family talks a lot, eats a lot, and they're very loud when they communicate. When you come to a family function, you're going to get a headache by the time you leave if you're not accustomed to this kind of conversation. There will always be enough food to feed 200 people even though only 20 were invited. You are expected to eat and talk. In fact, when we would bring guests over, we would have to prep them, "Hey, if you don't eat, and you don't talk, my family will think you're rude." Now, my wife's family is a lot different. Most of them don't share their opinions quickly. They try not to be gluttonous. So, what is rude? Talking or not talking? Eating or not eating? You see, it depends on the other person's perception. What is their perception? Rude is not a behavior, it is always a perception.

## Four Basic Patterns of Behavior

First seek to understand someone else's behavior, and they will likely understand yours. For at least ninety years, social scientists have worked on ways to explain why people do what they do. Back in 1928, William Moulton Martson wrote a book entitled *Emotions of Normal People* in which he introduced the concepts of will and a person's sense of power and their effect on personality and human behavior. Martson's work influenced the creation of the DISC model and other behavior assessments that cover the four basic patterns of people. Once you understand these patterns you can adapt to people; you can interpret their behavior differently. You create different perceptions of people. Once I understood this and how to read these different patterns in people, I also understood why certain people feel like they don't like me right away. It's because we have conflicting patterns.

## Drivers

The first pattern is called the Drivers. Drivers are bottom-line, no-nonsense, get to the point people. They are great delegators. They communicate with force. Their motto is ready, fire, aim. They can change quickly as long as it's tied to what they want. So they have no problem shifting gears, but they are so focused on their tasks that they tend to neglect people. Of all four styles, the Drivers are the worst listeners. However, there's a reason they don't listen; they don't have time and they already know what you're going to say! So, why listen? Do you know some Drivers in your life?

## Talkers

The second group is the Talkers. The Talker's goal in life is fun, excitement, visibility, and recognition. They tend to communicate with lots of stories that bring attention to their favorite subject—themselves. Their tone has lots of variance, and lots of volume. Talkers are so focused on the moment that they fail to plan long term. We can call them the TMI group, that is, the too much information group! They tend to lose sight of the details and think only in grand, big picture ways. The Talkers though, are very persuasive, and very influential. They have the ability to get others more excited about an idea than even they themselves are excited about. They are the only ones in the group that can win an argument without even really knowing what they're talking about.

## Thinkers

The third group is the Thinkers. The Thinkers are great planners and administrators. They value facts, logic, structure and information. If you want something done right, give it to a Thinker. If you want to have it done right away, well, think again because they tend to procrastinate getting finished until it's what? Perfect! They can be a little boring in their speech, monotonic, and analytical. They're very focused on eliminating flaws, so they tend to focus on what's wrong with the situation, with the project, with the company, than what's right. They're slow at change, slow at responses, and slow with communication. They might close their eyes if you ask them a question directly while they're downloading information. They're so focused on being perfect and right that many times they miss the whole point of the conversation.

## Feelers

The last group is the Feelers. They are great team players. The Feelers are your closest friends. They're the best listeners. They value close, personal one-to-one relationships. They want to get along with everyone and to do that, they avoid rocking the boat. The challenge is they're all heart. Imagine a heart with arms and legs, that's a Feeler. When there are decisions to be made, they just succumb to whatever their group wants to do. It's easy to hurt their feelings without even knowing it. Most of the time, if you hurt their feelings a little bit, they won't say anything, and they won't show it. However, when they get out of your sight, they will pull out their little book of hurts, turn to the page with your name on it and add a check mark. Too many times the Feelers are so supportive of everyone else that they neglect their own needs and feelings.

## Different Styles . . . Different Perceptions

Now, all of these styles can be perceived as rude. Your perception creates your reality. Remember the human behavior model? If you perceive one style as rude, then you interpret everything they do to support your perception. You then get emotional based on what you think they meant, and then you behave accordingly. The problem is different styles operate out of their own perceptions, and their motives are not your motives. Their needs are not your needs. Learn to meet their needs, and they'll respond to you differently.

For instance, the Drivers need results. They need to win, and they need to be in control. Let them drive. Let them steer. Let them decide. To get a Driver on board, start your phrases with, "Well, you seem to know what you're doing. So, what do you think?" You'll find that they will talk themselves into agreeing with you.

What do the Talkers need? They need attention, fun, applause, visibility, and recognition. They need speed, fast changes, and quick decisions. Don't delay too long. Let's go. Let's try something different. They may need to rearrange the furniture once in a while just to have a change. You know what they don't need? They don't need you to correct them in front of everyone. They're so focused on the audience noticing them, if you correct a Talker in front of an audience, they'll flip it and spin it on you, and it will go very badly. Never correct a Talker in front of their peers.

What do the Thinkers need? The Thinkers need low risk. They need to be correct. They need to have proof in order to be correct. Further, to prove it they need to have time to research every possible detail. You don't ask them for snap decisions because their answer will be no. You don't ask them if they like something. You ask them which decision would have the least amount of risk, and they can tell you that. You also put a time frame on it, "Hey, I'm going to ask you on Friday about A, B, C, or D so that will give you some time to take a look at it. Let me know which one has the most upside by Friday." You give them plenty of advance notice. They don't like pop quizzes.

What do the Feelers need? They need trust. They need relationship and community. They need authentic close personal rapport. They're not necessarily focused on winning or bringing attention to themselves. They just want to know that they can trust you. Do you like them genuinely? Remember, for Feelers it's all about authenticity. If you really understand Feelers and their needs, they'll be your friend for life.

*"Don't put diesel fuel in a Prius."* Dan Spacagna

From Gary Chapman's book *The Five Love Languages* we know there are five ways to fill someone's love tank or respect tank and they are:

- Acts of service
- Quality time
- Physical touch
- Words of affirmation
- Gifts

The challenge is most of the time we tend to show love according to how we like to receive love. That's equivalent to putting diesel fuel in a vehicle that runs on gasoline. It is still going to cost you $50 or $60 to put diesel in that car, but is it going to run? Are you going to get the benefit of the fuel? No. In fact, you're going to damage the car.

Let me give you an example of what I mean. Too many times we see dads only communicating in one love language: acts of service. Then the kid grows up and is on *Dr. Phil* accusing the dad of not loving him or her. The dad says something to the effect of, "What do you mean I didn't love you? I put you through college. I bought you everything you needed." The child, now an adult, responds, "Well, I never heard you once say that you loved me, and you were never home." If the child's love language is quality time, you can't buy that. You can't work into that. You have to be present. If his or her love language is words of affirmation, you have to say it.

For years, I would buy my wife expensive gifts. Why? That's' right, because I like expensive gifts! I would be disappointed when she wouldn't use them or wear them. But then I realized this truth after I read some books on this subject. I had been doing it wrong. Her type of love language involves words of affirmation, and she's a hugger, and that means more to her than an expensive gift. In fact, to this day, she has just about every note I've ever written her.

Pay attention to the people around you. What fuel do they run on? You can waste a lot of money and time and effort trying to get the behavior you want by filling a gasoline car with diesel fuel, but it's not going to run. Learn their language and then meet their need in the way they need it met.

What do we do to control behaviors? Well, using the four-style model, each style has their own go-to default moves to get what they want. The Drivers will typically threaten you and use force. The Talkers will bribe you or persuade you or maybe even fudge the truth. The Thinkers will administrate plan. They will organize their way into getting you to do something. The Feelers, well, they will just give in. They will do your work for you, or they will do it your way and then resent you.

## Rewards versus Threats

There are two basic ways that most people try to get other people to do what they want: rewards or threats. For example, managers try to get their employee's behavior to change by using rewards or threats. In one hand, they have a reward, and in the other hand, they have a consequence or a threat.

Rewards and threats do work temporarily, but they don't create long-term change. We know this because the fact is in the United States approximately 400,000 to 500,000 Americans get hired every month. Do you have an idea how many Americans quit their jobs in December of 2015? Would you be surprised to know that 3.1 million people quit in one month? On average, over 25 million Americans quit their jobs every year. Their salary—how much they make—has no influence on their decision, they still quit.

The top three reasons they quit have nothing to do with pay. It has to do with whether they like their boss, whether they feel appreciated by their boss, and if they feel like their work is important or rewarding. Rewards and threats create temporary motivation, but they don't last long term.

Threats are fear based. Many people believe that laws control behavior. There is no evidence to support this. Laws actually increase behavior. Laws reveal behavior. I have a lot of fun in my seminars. One of the things I'll do with a large seminar is hand out those ball-point pens that have the push button tabs. Then I'll make a rule at the beginning of the class. I'll say, "Please click your pen one time, and then don't click it during the rest of my class for the next six hours." You should watch people get uncomfortable with that rule and start secretly trying to click their pen throughout the day. Later, I will reveal the whole point of that experiment was to show them they didn't want to click their pens until I made the rule that they couldn't.

Here's another example, during Prohibition more women started drinking and going to speakeasies than they did before Prohibition. Previously, just men went to the bars, predominantly. During Prohibition, drinking increased among men and women because of a rule that prohibited drinking! America has more laws than most developed countries, and yet we have the highest prison population.

Threats and bribes are always short term. They don't change the behavior. They temporarily divert it. Focus on the behavior you want, and not the behavior you don't want.

We create images, because our minds are all visuals. For instance, if I told you "Don't slam the door on the way out of my office," what image did you have in your mind? That's right, an image of a slamming door. I have cognitively reinforced the behavior I do not want, not the behavior I want. So, what would be a better way to say that? "When you leave my office, close the door slowly." The image is reinforced.

## Will Power

Some people believe you can change behavior through willpower. I'm not here to tell you it's impossible. You can get off the horse; just drag it by the reins, off the trail. You can do things by willpower, but you're using only one-fifth of your brain power. The minute you stop the willpower you're going to go back to your old behavior.

Have you ever gotten in a vehicle that was a stick shift? Well, if you've ever owned one, then you know you always set the emergency brake or the parking brake. Have you ever driven off and forgotten to release the parking brake? Even though you give it more gas to keep the car moving, your engine has to work much harder. It would be smarter to release the brake and then without any more effort the car would go faster and further. We need to reprogram the unconscious to release the brakes it's holding back.

## Self-Disciplines

I use the phrase *self-disciplines* a lot. Discipline used to be a negative word to me, especially when it came to behavior. Discipline meant I was in trouble, and it was bad. My uncle was a Marine Sargent, and I thought of him as being disciplined, and it wasn't always in a positive light. He would wake up at 5:00 a.m. every day. He was always clean-cut and shaved. Because of my association with my uncle and discipline, whenever I heard the word discipline I had a negative reaction to it.

However, in one of my favorite books, one of my more ancient books I read on behavior, it teaches that self-discipline is something I can do by indirect effort that helps me do what I cannot do by direct effort. What I've learned is if you don't have willpower, and if you don't have the ability to stop a behavior, find the discipline that if you repeat it over and over will automatically reprogram the unconscious without will power. In other words, if you want to lift 200 lbs., and you can't, you shouldn't try to lift 200 lbs. the first time in the gym. You should start with 10 lbs. and lift it over and over again. Then, over time, 20 lbs. will be easier, and then 30, and so on. You get the idea. The discipline would lead to the outcome you want. It would make it impossible to fail. The only thing you have to do is commit 100% to the discipline. So self-disciplines have to be something you can do right now. They have to be really easy. I am into really passive disciplines that will yield high results.

For instance, if your round-trip commute to work totals 30 minutes, and you replace listening to music with listening to audio programs and audio books, you would read about 50 books a year just on the way to work and back. What would that do for your perception, for your skill set, for your career? Do you know anyone who reads 50 books a year? I know a few, and they are typically very high achievers.

How do you compare your efforts to your results to see if what you're doing is working? Typically there are four ways.

1. High efforts, high results. This is when you work really hard and get really good results. I don't ascribe to this way because over time high efforts, high results, leads to burnout.

The human psyche has an inner child. The inner child needs to relax at times, and it comes up to you and says, "Hey, can we relax? Can we have a little fun now?" You say, "No, we're busy. We can't do that." Your inner child goes away, then comes back a week later and says, "Can we have a little fun now?" You say, "No, no. We're too busy." If you keep doing that over and over, eventually, the inner child will break something. That's called the burnout. It will break your physical health, your mental health, your relationships, and your character. We all know people who work too hard and worked too long, and something snapped. That's high effort, high results.

2. High efforts and low results. That's when you understand passion a little. You have passion, but you don't have skill. Passion is only one-third of purpose. If you want to see passion without skill, you can go to karaoke any night of the week. That was me for over 30

years of my life. I was trying. It's just wasn't working out. That's high effort, low results.

3. Low efforts, low results. After expending all of that effort and getting low results, most people then drop to this level. They just give up. They become apathetic and in my opinion, it's why most people are looking for ways to numb their brain or their emotions through drugs or alcohol or food or television. It's really an apathetic disposition. They just don't care anymore.

4. Low efforts, high results. These are the things that are really easy to do and yield really high results.

## Disciplines of Engagement

Let's break this down into two categories: disciplines of engagement and disciplines of abstinence. If you have an attitude issue such as bitterness, unforgiveness, resentment, ungratefulness, you would want a discipline of engagement. This list will give some ideas:

- Serving at a homeless shelter
- Going on a mission trip
- Volunteering at a boy's or girls' club
- Signing up and committing to sing in the choir
- Being around those with greater needs than yours
- Going to men's group
- Going out on a weekend retreat.

These are all disciplines of engagements.

## Disciplines of Abstinence

If want to stop a compulsive behavior, I recommend using a discipline of abstinence such as fasting. There are many kinds of fasts, in fact, over 20. Most people just think of an absolute fast which is no food, just water. But you could fast, just on vegetables. You could fast from TV. During Lent, many people will fast from different things. So, create a discipline of abstinence. Silence or solitude would be a discipline of abstinence. Shutting off your cable for three months, and walking instead of driving to work are examples of disciplines of abstinence.

## Other Behavior Assessment Tools

Another behavior assessment tool is *Maslow's Hierarchy of Needs*. It looks like a pyramid. Abraham Maslow said you have to meet your physical needs first, which is the bottom of the pyramid. You then meet your security needs as you move up the pyramid, on to relational needs, and then esteem needs. Self-actualization is at the top of the pyramid. A self-actualized person is the most creative, secure and peaceful. I like to think of it differently. At the top, you are 100% who you're supposed to be regardless of what anyone else says, even your parents. You are operating in your purpose.

# The Power of Flaws

## The Golden Buddha

Many years ago in Thailand, monks were moving this giant Buddha statue, and it weighed many tons. It was made of clay and was an icon of their religion and their history.

During the move, the monk in charge stumbled and the statue fell off of one of the lifts and cracked. Imagine being that monk in charge of this move! This thing is priceless. It's an icon of their history. It's irreplaceable and he just damaged it. So, they stopped moving it. He was so distraught he couldn't sleep that night.

It started to rain and he thought, "Oh, great. This is perfect. Now, it's raining." So they covered it up with a tarp. Throughout the night he would go out to survey the damage and to make sure it was staying dry. Every time he saw a damaged area he went into a stress response. He was looking at the damage under the moonlight and noticed light reflecting back at him. He thought, well, this is solid clay, what is reflecting back? Clay doesn't reflect light.

The next day, he told some of the other monks what happened. They had an idea. They chiseled away on the back side where it wouldn't show, and what they uncovered after they chipped away about a foot of clay was a solid 10,000 pound golden Buddha!

Several hundred years prior—I think it was when the Burmese attacked Thailand—the monks got wind of it, so they covered up this Golden Buddha with a foot of clay, and decorated and painted it to make it look less valuable. Since all the monks were annihilated, there was no one left to tell anyone, "Hey after the war, by the way, uncover the Buddha. It's solid gold." So, he discovered this through a "mistake."

I think the story of the golden Buddha represents a lot of people. The golden Buddha is you and me; it's our self-actualized person, with all the potential, and all the creativity we have. We get covered up with layers of stuff (mud and garbage), through the ups and downs of life. Self-discovery isn't re-creating one's self; it's just uncovering what was always there.

## Diamonds Are Flawed

Imagine I had a 10-carat diamond. Most people have a perceived value of diamonds. What if I took it and put it in a ball of manure. If I were to offer it to you, would still want it? I'm sure you would because you know it has value! That's how I look at people. It's worth getting my hands dirty because there's value on the inside. So, you're the diamond, but the manure is all the stuff you go through. Maybe it's all the self-esteem issues you may have. It may be hang-ups from your past, or some habits you've acquired that are not helpful. No one wants to go out into the world and say, "Hi, my name is _____. I'm a ball of crap." What most people do is they cover up the manure with nail polish or hairspray or a Mercedes Benz, or something expensive. For example, they try to get the right job or have the right relationship to add to their perceived value. They don't understand that they don't have to add anything to create value; rather, they may need to take something away.

If I were to give you this diamond in a ball of manure, you would go ahead and get your fingers dirty to get the diamond. Then you would take it to a jeweler to verify its authenticity. The jeweler would look for a flaw because the jeweler knows if that diamond has no flaw, it's fake. It's a cubic zirconia. Every diamond has a flaw, and it's the flaw which gives it value. We're taught incorrectly to cover up our flaws, and not to talk about our pains and our problems. I'm here to tell you that your flaws are actually what make you valuable and powerful. They are what give you authenticity. They give you power to speak into someone else's life. Stop hiding your flaws.

## The Story of Roger Crawford

Roger Crawford was born with one leg and pretty much no hands. His parents believed in instilling high self-esteem, and they asked Roger what he wanted to do with his life. He said, "Well, I think I'm an athlete. I see myself as an athlete and that's what I want to be." His parents said, "Well, you're going to have to work at it. You're going to have to get good at it." Notice that they didn't tell Roger he couldn't be an athlete. Roger always believed he was an athlete. That was his diamond. They didn't let all the garbage—the manure of his disability—stop him. So they got him a prosthetic leg, and he learned how to run and do all the things required of an athlete. He made the high school football team. He played all four years in high school with one leg and no hands.

His senior year his dad asked him, "Hey, Roger. What's your goal this year?" Roger said, "Well, I'd love to catch a touchdown." He said, "Why is that important?" Roger said, "Well, when you catch a touchdown, the girls go crazy for you, and I would really enjoy that." His dad said, "Do you have any skill?" Passion is not enough. You need passion plus skill. Then his dad asked, "Could you catch a ball and run with it?" Roger said, "Well, it doesn't matter. They'll never throw me the ball." You see, Roger was a defensive lineman, and they don't throw the ball to defensive linemen. His dad, "Well, you have to be prepared if you want to accomplish your goal." So, every day his dad came home and threw the football with Roger, and he learned how to catch. After he learned how to catch, he learned how to run and do all these juke moves and all those cool things, but the quarterback never threw him the ball because he was a defensive lineman.

It was the last game he played in high school. The quarterback dropped back, and Roger rushed the quarterback as he always did. Another player hit the quarterback's arm as he went to throw the ball, and the ball went straight up in the air. When Roger looked up and saw that ball, he knew if he could get under it, he could catch it, and if he could catch it, he knew he could run. Sure enough, he got under the ball, and he caught it. Then he took off for the end zone. He got to about the three-yard line and someone grabbed his left leg from behind. He pulled. Roger pulled. Roger said, "My leg came off, and I hopped the rest of the way into the end zone." He said, "Much better than scoring the touchdown, was the look on the defender's face holding half of a leg."

Roger went on to play tennis in college. The challenge with that is the first rule of tennis is to have a good firm grip. Roger has no hands. So he used duct tape to tape the racket to his arms. Roger lost one match in college to a guy named John

McEnroe. If you want to find a reason not to do something, there are plenty of reasons out there. There's plenty of negativity. However, you need to ask yourself, "How can I do this?"

What makes Roger's story so powerful is the fact that he has flaws. He has one leg and no hands. If he looked like one of these super athletes, six foot six, 250 pounds with muscles everywhere, yes, it would still be a good story, but not as powerful. Your power comes from your flaws.

## Create Cognitive Dissonance

Expect to feel uncomfortable. Create structural tension or cognitive dissonance for what you want. Put yourself in an atmosphere that supports your new mindset. Put yourself in an atmosphere that will make it hard to fail. If you're trying to lose weight, and you hang around people with beer bellies, it will be easier to fail. Hang around people with six packs. You'll find yourself automatically behaving like them.

Sleep in your workout clothes. I met a woman at one of my trainings who was in her 60's. She lost 90 pounds late in life. One of the tricks she used was putting on her workout clothes at night, and leaving her shoes at the foot of her bed with the laces pulled out. So, when she got up each morning her feet would go right into her shoes, and then mentally she would think, "Well, I'm pretty much almost done at this point; I might as well do it."

Use your physiology to give yourself an advantage. Allow yourself to be uncomfortable. Your discomfort will change. You will adapt. Choose to sit in a different seat. Eat at a different table. Talk to a different person. Go to a different restaurant.

Imagine you have already achieved and overcome what you want to achieve and overcome. Ask yourself, what one thing made the biggest impact in accomplishing this? And then commit 100% to the one discipline that would give you that skill or ability. Meditate for 15 minutes in the morning or at night. Pre-live your day and see it going perfectly. Think about what you want, rather than what you don't want. Use your imagination for success instead of worry.

# Stress to Success Action Steps

*Commit to applying what you have learned in this chapter before you move on to the next chapter! Make it stick!*

### EFFECTIVE WAYS TO MODIFY BEHAVIOR

- Take a behavior assessment. If you've never taken a DISC assessment, you can find a free assessment at www.123test.com/dis-personality-test. Of all the tools out on the web, I like *DISC, Colors Assessments* and *The Platinum Rule* to accomplish learning your style and how to adapt to others.

- Learn to use low and high Intensity. Always use low intensity when reprimanding yourself or others for unproductive behavior. Always use high intensity for praise for productive behaviors. (Parents and bosses usually have this backwards).

## SEVEN STEPS TO GET WHAT YOU WANT

1. Wake up one hour earlier than you normally do. Read a book related to your field 30 to 60 minutes daily.
2. Rewrite your 10 goals every day to program them in your subconscious and activate your super conscious mind.
3. Plan every day in advance. This increases your output by 25% immediately.
4. Set priorities and concentrate on the most valuable use of your time.
5. Listen to audio programs in your car. Shut off the radio and the advertising, and the music that you don't even like.
6. Ask yourself the two magic questions:

    - What did I do right?
    - What would I do differently next time?

This reinforces your positive self-esteem and predisposes you to adjust in the next situation and not quit.

Treat every person you meet like they are a million dollar customer.

CHAPTER SIX

# Beliefs: The Master Key

*"There is nothing with which every man is so afraid as getting to know how enormously much he's capable of doing and becoming."* Søren Kierkegaard

*"Whether you think you can or you think you can't, you're right."* Henry Ford

*"For as he thinketh in his heart, so is he."* Proverbs 23:7

You have made it to Chapter Six: The Master Key. Let's recap what you've learned so far. Our *human behavior model* shows us that emotion is not the first thing that happens after events. We have a perception of what we think we see, hear, or experience, and that perception is largely filtered. We then interpret what we think we saw, heard or experienced. We typically have one of three interpretations; this is good for me; this is bad for me; or this does not affect me, it's indifferent. Our brain then creates emotion to support the perceived event and interpretation. Lastly, in the E plus R equals O model (Events plus Response equal Outcome), behavior is the most immediate cause of outcomes.

What is the master key that would circumvent all of this? What would override all perceptions, all interpretations, all emotions and all behavior? Most people try to manage their behavior, which would change their outcomes. Some try to manage their emotions, which would change their behaviors. Others change their interpretations and say things are good when they're not, and yet others change or increase their perception of the world. However, the thing that unlocks all of this is belief. Belief overrides all emotions, perceptions, interpretations and behaviors. Once you know and master your beliefs, everything else changes.

Imagine watching a sporting event on TV. In a previous chapter I mentioned my home team playing game seven in a best of seven series. When I don't believe I know the outcome, my emotions go up and down and can be very negative at times. However, if I know it's scripted or the event already happened—that is, the outcome has already been determined—I can watch it and watch failures happen within the game and not have as intense negative emotions.

I'm reminded of a young author who won all kinds of awards in high school. She got a full-ride scholarship to a university for creative writing. Her whole life she loved writing and was told she was very good at it . . . that is, until her first major assignment in college. A visiting professor from Harvard University was assisting with the class, and he gave her a failing grade on her the assignment. She was shocked and challenged him. She asked him, "What happened? Why did I fail?" The Harvard professor said, "You're no good. You cannot write." She questioned him, "What do you mean?" He systematically picked her assignment apart and told her "You're no good." She was worried that she would fail her course, which would then disqualify her for the rest of her scholarship. The professor made a deal with her. He said, "I will give you a passing grade if you change your major." Out of fear, she changed her major and finished college.

Fifteen years later, a movie was being filmed on location in her hometown. Everyone in the town went to see the movie stars. However, this now middle-aged woman went looking for the writers. One of the writers asked her, "Why are you hanging out with us? Everyone's here to see the movie stars." She said, "I always wanted to be a writer." He asked her why she doesn't write. She told him the story about what happened in college. He said, "What does one professor know? I write for a living." He gave her his business card, and said, "Why don't you write something and send it to me? I'll tell you if it's any good."

It took her a year to write the first novel, and it was called *Romancing the Stone*. They loved it, and it became a motion picture. For 15 years, Catherine Lanigan let one person create a belief that she was no good, and it affected every part of her life. It affected her use of her talent. It affected her happiness. It affected her performance. Once her beliefs changed, she then went on to write many other books that were also made into movies. You see, what you believe about yourself will override everything you experience.

## Two Types of Beliefs

As we continue to examine beliefs, like Catherine Lanigan you will discover that the beliefs you hold about yourself can override everything you experience. A bit later in this chapter I will talk more about beliefs—about the big picture, about life and about the meaning of everything. For now, we're going to separate beliefs into two types: functional beliefs and dysfunctional beliefs.

## Functional Beliefs

Functional beliefs are always based on hard facts and hard evidence proving them. Everyone can see these facts, and the facts are objective. When you operate in a functional belief, it leads to a productive emotional state. In other words, it creates love-based emotions. Functional beliefs are logical, so no matter who does the research every person will reach the same conclusion.

## Dysfunctional Beliefs

Dysfunctional beliefs are based on feelings or personal logic. They lead to an unproductive emotional state, and they are typically sourced out of fear-based emotions. Dysfunctional beliefs have no supporting evidence.

# How Unconscious Beliefs Affect Behavior and Emotion

You can have functional beliefs, and you can have dysfunctional beliefs. You can also be aware of your beliefs or unaware of your beliefs, that's why it's important to separate functional and dysfunctional from conscious or unconscious beliefs.

Let's look at how an unconscious belief affects behavior and emotion. A friend of ours was a former professional basketball player who broke his arm in a motorcycle accident in the prime of his career. In desperate attempts to play basketball again, he had a number of surgeries and was promised full use of his arm. The therapy was tremendously painful and very grueling. After many failed attempts to fix his arm, he became depressed so his wife bought him a unicycle to take his mind off of the rehab. The unicycle required tremendous focus to master, and he got so good at riding this unicycle that he began performing during half-time at the basketball games and giving speeches.

One of his routines was challenging the crowd to a one-up contest. He would do different things on the unicycle like shooting baskets and then would create more difficult challenges to shock the crowd. His grand finale was always putting someone on his shoulders and then doing the same tricks. That was the one where people just couldn't believe he'd be able to do it. And so, he would cause them to doubt that he could do it, and then he would put someone on his shoulders and then do his routine perfectly. The crowd would cheer and go wild for this great feat that he accomplished.

After the finale, he would ask the crowd, "Do you now believe that I can do all these things? Do you believe that I can put someone on my shoulders and ride them all around and do these tricks?" The crowd yelled resoundingly, "Yes, we believe." He then asked for one person among the crowd to get down there and prove their belief and get on his shoulders. The interesting thing about this challenge is in all these years, no one has ever come down to prove their belief because most people think "seeing is believing." But the fact is they had an unconscious belief that stopped them. The greater unconscious belief was that they would get injured, or that he was not capable of doing it again.

You can say you believe things are going to work out for your good, but if you feel nervous, or if you have fear-based emotions, you have an unconscious disbelief that's stronger than the fact. So, seeing is not necessarily believing. When your beliefs are both conscious and unconscious, your body won't create unproductive emotions. The rule is that your body cannot lie. If it's feeling nervous, it's because you have a fear-based belief either consciously or unconsciously. Dysfunctional beliefs create fear-based unproductive emotions that are not supported by facts.

One of the hardest questions you'll ever be asked is "Should bad things happen to good people?" If we use our functional and dysfunctional model, there will be two answers. You could say no or you could say yes. Now, most people would say, no; bad things should not happen to good people. The next few questions you want to ask are, "Why? What facts do you have to support that? Do you have any facts to support the belief that bad things should not happen to good people?"

Since the beginning of recorded history, if you believe the first family were Adam and Eve, their kids killed each other and so on. Generation after generation, people have been killing each other. Countries have been at war against each other's tribes and races. Earthquakes and natural disasters have happened. The facts are since the beginning of time, things that could be seen as bad have been happening to all kinds of people. There are no facts to support the belief that they shouldn't happen.

Let me ask how you would feel if you had the belief that bad things should never happen to you, and then they do? Would you not be shocked? Wouldn't you be afraid? Wouldn't you feel hurt? Well, these are all unproductive fear-based emotions. By definition, because you have no facts to support your belief, and because it produces fear-based and unproductive emotions, this is a dysfunctional belief. There's no supporting evidence to prove that bad things shouldn't happen to you.

Let's examine the opposite end of this discussion. Should bad things happen to good people? You could say yes. The next question is, "Why? What are the supporting facts?" Well, bad things have been happening. "Bad" things do happen. Now, if I had the belief that, yes, bad things could happen to me, how do I feel most days when they don't happen? I feel grateful. I feel blessed. I'm not promised a problem-free life, yet here I am in the wealthiest country in the world. I have three kids and a wife who loves me, and I'm not guaranteed tomorrow. I savor the moment today. Are those emotions productive or unproductive? Gratitude, love, hope, and peace are pretty productive emotions.

## Self-Concept: The Dysfunctional and Functional Models in Action

Using the formula for dysfunctional and functional models, it's more functional to believe that bad things could happen to you. One of the self-beliefs that override your performance, your ability to get results and your confidence, is called your self-concept. The self-concept is really a whole bundle of different belief systems that you have about yourself. I'm going to break it down into three parts.

## Part One: Self-Esteem

The first part is your self-esteem. Your self-esteem is your ability to like yourself. Not a like on *Facebook* where you just click "like" rather your real ability to be okay with you and to enjoy who you are. In Gloria Steinem's research, she found that two out of three people in North America have a low self-esteem. Only one out of three adults like and esteem themselves. Many think it's just the homeless or unemployed that struggle with low self-esteem, but the reality is it's the people in your home, office and school. Every day there are events that can affect your self-esteem. In any life event, your self-esteem could do one of three things. It can go up. It can go down, or it can be unaffected.

Before I talk about what events do, I want you to understand the poker chip theory of self-esteem as explained by Jack Canfield. Self-esteem and life can be compared to playing poker and the amount of poker chips you have. If you have a lot of poker chips, you can take a lot of losses and stay in the game. However, if you have a few poker chips, any loss is major failure and can cause you a lot of anxiety. Imagine, you go into a poker game with a thousand dollars. You could play loosely. You could lose five hands in a row, and it wouldn't bother you. You'd keep playing. You'd stay in the game. You would even have a good time in the process.

On the other hand, if I were playing poker and had only $50 that I borrowed from my car payment and lost two $20 hands in a row, I would be anxious. Could you imagine the nervousness, the fear, the anxiety? It's not the amount of the loss that I experienced; rather it's the fact that I don't have a lot of poker chips. It's not getting fired that makes you feel bad. It's the amount of self-esteem you have when you get fired.

There are a lot of events that affect our ability to have high self-esteem. I mentioned earlier that in any event your self-esteem could go up, be unaffected, or go down. When people graduate from high school, their self-esteem will usually go down. In fact, research suggests that self-esteem drops to about 45% in boys, and it drops even lower in girls. Many times, it's because of peer pressure. It's because of prom or whether they even go to prom. Many high school graduates don't have plans after high school, and it causes them not to feel good about themselves.

Another example is graduating from law school. Some of the Ivy League schools have done studies and found that if you go to their law school, your self-esteem will be at its lowest when you graduate. You may be in debt. You may have been embarrassed by professors who called you out when you didn't know the answers to the questions in the class. You may graduate from college unsure about yourself, your abilities, and your future more than ever before. The things we think drive our self-esteem up can actually drive it down. Are your routines making you feel better about yourself or worse?

## Self-Talk

Let's take a look at one of the factors of self-esteem, and that's self-talk. If you change what you say to yourself, you change the outcome. In other words, imagine you were in one of my seminars with a thousand people in attendance. Right in front of a thousand people I called you out, and I said, "You know what? I have taught in almost every state in the United

States and all across North America. I have taught over 30,000 people, and you keep asking the dumbest questions." If I called you out like that in front of all of your peers, do you think your self-esteem would take a hit there? Would it go down?

Well, let's apply E plus R equals O thinking. Identify the event that triggered the self-esteem going down. What was the event? The event was I insulted you publicly. What did you think the outcome was? If you said the outcome was that your self-esteem would go down; that's not the right response. What did we skip? That's right; we skipped the response because most people don't respond out loud. They respond internally. They talk to themselves. Right now, you may be talking to yourself. The fact is we have 55,000 self-talks on average, every day. Most people are aware of less than ten percent of them.

What if I insulted you, and said, "You're the dumbest person I've ever trained." If you said to yourself, "How did it take him this long to figure that out? Most people know right away." In that situation, your self-esteem would probably go down even further.

What if I made the same insult and said, "You are dumb," and you said to yourself, "Who is this seminar trainer who would insult someone he doesn't even know?" Your self-esteem wouldn't be affected because it wasn't ever questioned.

What if I insulted you and said, "You are the dumbest person I've ever trained." And you talked to yourself, and said, "This has happened to me before. I'm very good looking, very intelligent, very outgoing, and most of these seminar trainers know that, and they get intimidated by me. Dan's been looking my way quite a bit; maybe he has a crush on me." If that was your self-talk, what would the outcome be? Would your self-esteem go up? Would it be unaffected? Or would it go down?

The fact is, any event can create any outcome. Let me repeat that again. Any event can create any outcome. One of the keys is you have to change the way you talk to yourself. You see, it's not what people say to you; it's what you say to yourself that creates your emotion or your self-esteem. Your self-esteem is your responsibility. Stop the negative self-talk. Commit to say only positive things about yourself to yourself. If your friends talked to you the way you talk to yourself, how long would you keep them as friends?

## Part Two: Self-Image

The second part to the self-concept belief system is your self-image. Your self-image is the inner mirror you look into before you go into any kind of event, especially a job interview, a proposal, or something where you're on the spot. When you have a positive inner mirror, you walk positively, you feel confident, and you tend to have more success. When you have a negative inner mirror, you tend to lose confidence, lose energy and put out a negative vibe which challenges your success. Always choose to see yourself in the best light. It's not what is; it's what you choose to see.

If you look at people with eating disorders like anorexia, it's not that they're overweight; rather, it's that they cannot see that they're not. I bet you know some beautiful people who believe they're ugly, and it affects their confidence and their ability to have relationships. It's their inner mirror that's the problem, not the reality.

You can circumvent this problem if you create cognitive dissonance for yourself. If you only look at airbrushed people in Cosmopolitan magazines and television shows, and then you look in the mirror, you're going to create a dissonance against yourself. Find a way to see yourself in a positive light. Fall in love with one part of you at a time.

The rule is, if you're surrounded by people you don't like then you don't like yourself. Your inner mirror will reflect back what you think about yourself. If you are annoyed by idiots, you see yourself as an idiot. This is both challenging and liberating. It was challenging for me to realize at one point in my life, I didn't see myself positively. It's liberating to know that I cannot be annoyed by anything in someone else that isn't already there in me.

### Part Three: Self-Ideal

The third part is your self-ideal. Your self-ideal is your bundle of values and beliefs about the best possible version of you. This helps you make decisions in the moment. The key to having a really strong self-ideal is to clarify and identify what you value and then never compromise it. Most people don't know what they value. They make decisions based on other people, or based on trends, or based on culture. The fact is that people who are very successful are very clear about who they are and what they do and do not value. So again, the key is to identify and clarify what you stand for and then never compromise.

It's 100% or zero. Remember the 99%? Integrity is a connection between my behavior and my beliefs. When I have integrity, it has to be 100% so that people can trust my decisions. It also shortens the amount of time it takes me to decide. Yes, carrying out a decision might take some time. It might take some skill to tell someone 'no' with tact, but the decision itself is easy. I know what I stand for, and I know what I don't stand for.

Decide now not *what* you want to be but *who* you want to be. Create a "best version" of you. Make your decisions from the perspective of your ideal self.

# Stress to Success Action Steps

*Commit to applying what you have learned in this chapter before you move on to the next chapter! Make it stick!*

Take some time to answer the following questions:

1. If your behavior was all that people saw, what would they accuse you of believing?

2. What do your calendar and your checking account reveal about your values?

3. What are your big rocks?

4. Do your big rocks really matter to you?

5. How are you putting them first?

6. What is your why?

7. Why do you believe what you believe?

8. Are there any facts to support it?

9. Could you defend your beliefs with logic and facts?

10. Are they functional or dysfunctional?

11. If you maintain these beliefs, do they produce positive or negative emotions?

12. Why are those beliefs important to you?

# CHAPTER SEVEN

# The Three P's

"*All things are subject to interpretation. Whichever interpretation prevails at a given time is a function of power and not truth.* Friedrich Nietzsche

"*We cannot solve today's problems with the same kind of thinking that created them.*" Albert Einstein

The three P's of purpose are passion, profession and production. The goal in life is to spend as much time, talent and treasure in all three areas of your life. This will create productive emotions, perpetual happiness and peace in your life regardless of circumstances. The beauty of this system is the more pain and problems in your life, the more qualified you become to operate in the center of your purpose. Remember, the manure— the perceived unpleasant events in your life—is great fertilizer for your purpose. The key is to embrace the painful parts of your life, interpret them to work out for your good while believing you are becoming who you were always meant to be.

## What Is Purpose?

Purpose is more than just passion, and it's more than financial success. Purpose is fulfilled when all three are operating in harmony. Before we go over the details of the three P's let's discuss why having a purpose is so important to your life, family and business.

In the business world, purpose is what keeps employees from leaving a company and is what allows us to persevere in tough times. We know that on average 2 million Americans voluntarily quit their job every 30 days, which costs employers millions of dollars every year in lost productivity and HR expenses. According to the U. S. Department of Labor, the cost of a "bad hire" can equal up to 30% of that employee's first year earnings! Why are so many quitting? I believe it's largely due to lack of purpose. Pareto's 80/20 principle is best applied to workers in that 20% of employees do 80% of the work, and 80% give a 20% effort. So why do some employees do so much while other employees just drift by? I believe it comes from a failure to connect an individual's personal purpose to the purpose of the organization. Researchers have found the top three reasons employees quit their jobs are:

1. They don't like their boss/manager.
2. They don't feel respected or appreciated.
3. They feel their work is meaningless or in other words, has no purpose.

Purpose is what makes difficult work worth the effort. Think about some of the tragedies of our recent times such as

9-11 or the many hurricanes that devastated our coastal communities. The one common denominator is that many people rush to Ground Zero to work in horrible conditions for free! The working conditions are some of the worst imaginable, yet thousands rush to offer aid because of the value of the work.

If an employee perceives there is no purpose or value in the work of an organization, the employee will lose interest and motivation. It has been documented that the Nazis tortured concentration camp prisoners with many unusually cruel routines. One such torture involved moving giant piles of scrap and rubbish from one side of the camp to the other using only manual labor. It would take days and many man-hours to accomplish the task. The real torture began once the prisoners thought they were finished. The guards would then command them to put it right back where it was when they started. Over and over the Nazis would reinforce to the prisoners that their work was futile and meaningless. Adult men lost hope, and some broke down mentally and physically during these rituals. Once a person has no purpose, he or she has no hope.

Many organizations fail to share the vision and purpose of their organization in a meaningful way with their employees. I heard about a manager scheduled to attend a motivational seminar but wanted to play golf for the day instead. The manager arrived over an hour before the seminar started, dressed for golf and let the trainer know that he would not be attending the seminar because it was not a requirement for his position, and he could not be fired for not attending. The trainer asked the manager why he showed up so early to tell him he would not be attending the seminar. He also asked the manager if there was something he wanted to know before leaving. The manager said, "Well, there is one thing. How can I motivate my employees?" The trainer smiled and assured him that he could answer the question quickly, and it would not interfere with his golf plans. The manager was now eager to hear the words of wisdom from the trainer. The trainer replied simply, "You cannot." The manager showed irritation and asked how that could be true if they teach six-hour seminars on motivation. The trainer replied that motivation is internal and manipulation is external. If the employee does not want to do the right thing, you cannot make them become motivated. Most managers want to manipulate people and there are two basic ways they do it, through reward or threat, as mentioned earlier.

First, let's discuss the reward. The manager creates an incentive to entice the employee to do what the manager wants done. Notice, the employee still does not desire to do the task but has only one choice if he or she wants the reward. This works temporarily, but will never produce long-term results because it fails to produce internal desire or motivation from the employee.

The second option for most managers is the threat. The threat is also manipulation because it leaves the employee without a choice. The employee may go along with the wishes of the manager temporarily, but once again it's an external manipulation of behavior without internal motivation. What you have to ask yourself as a leader is, "Do I want people to do what I want, or do I want them to *want* to do what I want?" Employees who do not want to do the right thing will find a way to avoid it regardless of threats and bribery. Employees who want to do the right thing will find a way to make it happen regardless of circumstances. Which kind of employees would you rather have, those who are manipulated temporarily or those who are motivated from within? A motivated employee will not leave you over a few dollars per hour or the latest ergonomic desk and computer chair.

## The Three Areas of Purpose

Let's look at the three areas of purpose and how you can move closer to becoming everything you were meant to be regardless of your past.

### Passion

What is passion? Some say it's everything; I disagree. Passion is one-third of the equation. Passion plus skill gets you closer to your purpose, but passion alone is not enough. Have you ever gone out to a karaoke club? Typically there are many passionate people who sign up to sing and get their five minutes in the spotlight, but few of them are very good. Passion alone isn't enough, but it's the start of your purpose. Passion without any skill as a vocalist might get you to week one of *American Idol* or *The Voice*. I know passion is important, but just telling someone to "follow their passions alone" might be setting them up for frustration.

So how do you know what your passion is? Your passion is connected to your inner most being. You'll know when you're operating in your passion because money has nothing to do with your motivation to do it. In fact, many people work five days a week to do what they're passionate about on the weekends. People will finance their passions if they have to.

When you are operating in your passion, you might be tired, but you're not stressed. In fact, the opposite is true. Your passion makes you feel alive. It may be something that you have a "natural" attraction to. It may be something that grabs your heart every time you're near it. Sometimes it's an area that you've been told you are a natural at doing. If money were no object, what would you do with your time?

Most people have buried their passions in grade school and have settled for what was socially programmed into them by society, their parents or teachers. If you were financially secure, and after you splurged on a vacation and the newest luxury item, what would you do, then? What do you have a genuine interest in? That is your passion. It could be a cause or a "hobby." It could be a situation like being in leadership or speaking to large groups. It could be a special interest group or your family. Your passion can also change over time, and as your awareness of self increases.

Years ago, I would have told you my passion was performing music. While I still enjoy music I discovered that I really enjoyed what my music did for people. I was passionate about how it affected and changed people. I loved communicating through music, but my passion was illumination. Now, I use my words and stories to illuminate through speaking in seminars, coaching and training. I still use music as a medium, but it's the result that is my passion, not the tool. I would happily talk about personal development and emotional health anytime, to anyone, anywhere for free.

A while back, I took Uber to the airport. The driver and I began a conversation, and he asked me what I speak about. It was only a 20-minute drive, but our conversation moved very quickly to the point where he explained he was recently given a prescription to treat a physical symptom. I shared with him the stats on prescription-drug use, and he told me that his wife (born in Columbia) was shocked when the doctor told him to take the prescription for the rest of his life as this is not normal in their country. As the conversation moved along I noticed that we were close to the airport, so I asked him to go through a drive-through, so I could order breakfast and extend our conversation. Even though I was paying the Uber driver premium rates to continue this conversation, I did it because I value people's lives. When I'm operating in my passion, my motivation is not reliant on income.

How much time do you spend in your passion? Most people "live for the weekends." We use expressions like "TGIF" and "Sunday/Fun-day." Frankly, if five out of the seven days of your life are meaningless, then you have a sad life. If 70% of your life is done because you "have to" or is something you don't value, that is sad. If you woke up today you've been given the same 24 hours that everyone else who woke up received. It's not owed to any of us, but we can choose to operate in our passions. It's not always about quitting your job and doing your hobby for a living. You do need to move closer to your passion, or you will lose your heart's motivation and inspiration. Remember, the word inspiration literally means to "breathe into." When you are inspired, you are breathing life into your passion!

If I planted an acorn from an oak tree next to a forest of pine trees, what would it become? Don't over think it. It would become an oak tree. Unfortunately, we have many oak trees that dress like pine trees. They're operating apart from their design and giftedness and they're usually miserable. Sure many have decent incomes (remember if you make at least $25k/year USD you're in the top 2% of income earners in the world), but they're not living in their purpose. Find what it is that makes you come alive and commit to spending more time in it. Hang out with oak trees and watch what sparks inside of you. Fan the spark into a flame and you'll be amazed how all of your previous struggles align with the realization of your passion. Passion is not the only thing, but it's the beginning of discovering your purpose.

Remember the golden Buddha from chapter five? Purpose is kind of like that golden Buddha statue, it's already in there, but past hurts and outside influences are covering it up. In turn, your self-esteem plummets, and you don't believe there is anything of value inside of you. Many people then try to cover up the "clay" with a layer of false good, such as better cars, hair and other externals that don't create real joy. I'm here to tell you that there are no mistakes. Just like that monk, if you embrace responsibility and look for the greater good you will discover that all things work together to bring you into your ultimate purpose. The value is already there we just have to uncover it. This "mistake" uncovered one of the most valuable golden statues ever discovered.

Embrace your "flaws" or "mistakes." Take 100% responsibility for who you are *now* and you will discover that your passion will illuminate your life like never before. The alternative is to allow fear to stifle you and never discover the golden version of you that was always there.

Self-discovery is not creating you; it's revealing what you were always meant to be. My hope is that you'll embrace who you are and fan the spark of your passion into a flame. Then you're ready to add skill to it, and that takes you to the next part of purpose, which is profession. Passion plus profession moves you towards your purpose.

## Profession

Passion is a great start but passion plus skill is the key to fulfilling your purpose. You may love to sing, but if you never develop the ability, you're headed towards a false good or narcissism at best. In our 3 C's of perpetual happiness, it takes contribution, continuing growth, and community to maintain lasting happiness. The last P, profession can help you to accomplish these.

Develop your skills so that they produce results that are beneficial to others. This will build your self-esteem and grow your courage. If your passion is singing, then take lessons and never stop learning from those who are better than you. As a musician, I had a mentor who confronted me with the fact that I was not developing my skills regularly. I defended my position stating I didn't need lessons due to my years of experience playing music on stage. My mentor informed me that artists like Celine Dion and others have vocal coaches and get instructions regularly. I never forgot his next question: "Are you better than they are?" There was no doubt about the answer, I wasn't. If the best of the best need coaches and instruction, then what made me think I didn't?

The reality is most of us neglect developing our ability because we're afraid that we will find out we're frauds. Once again, we make decisions sourced from the unproductive emotion of fear. The fact is what gets measured gets improved.

How do your skills measure up? You may have a lot or a little talent but what have you done with it? In five years, you'll be older, but will you be better? Commit to developing your skills regardless of age, and you'll produce results that benefit others.

All business skills are learnable. When it comes to fulfilling your purpose in business there really is no excuse for avoiding professional development. You can learn just about any business skill in the comfort of your home or office. There are online tutorials and webinars available 24 hours a day.

### Automobile University

I want to go into more detail regarding an idea I introduced you to in chapter five. Create your own university in your car! If you drive at least 30 minutes to work each day, then you have enough time to read 50 audio books per year. That's just Monday through Friday on the drive to and from work. What would reading or listening to 50 books a year do for your skill set? I'm willing to bet less than 5% of your associates read 50 books a year. That would immediately put you in the top 5% of people in your circle.

I have replaced music and talk radio and now listen primarily to audio books and seminar CDs and have listened to some of my favorite psychology books over 10 times! I've listened to other books more than 20 times, and there are a few books that I've read or listened to so often that I could not even guess the count. Imagine what this kind of repetition would do for you! There are smartphone apps like Audible.com and Audiobooks.com that make it easy to access thousands upon thousands of titles for as little as $15 a month.

## CANEI

The CANEI formula was created by Japanese manufacturers and it stands for: Constant And Never-Ending Improvement. In the today's competitive marketplace you're either updating your skills or you're becoming outdated. Those who thrive in this economy are resolved to develop their abilities and skills to match the ever-changing needs of their clients and customers. They work at this constantly.

### Updated or Outdated

Several years ago the largest home video rental company decided to stop adapting to the market. It was sold to a large media conglomerate because of that decision. Blockbuster Video was the leader in home movie rentals. Did you have a Blockbuster card? I did. Yet, a decade later Blockbuster no longer exists. Why? Did the market dissolve? Do people no longer rent movies and T.V. shows today? Blockbuster Video didn't adapt to the changing demands of their clients causing Netflix and Redbox to take Blockbuster's market share. Although Netflix and Redox rent movies, they do it differently. They adapted to the demands of the customer and now they own the market. If you're not updated, then you're outdated. Successful people have a mindset to never stop improving. There is no shortage of examples of organizations that have become irrelevant because they did not practice CANEI.

### Relationships Influence Your Growth

Three relationships you should have in your life to maintain CANEI are a mentor, an associate and a protégé. If you are the smartest person in your circle of friends, then your circle is too small. Many people surround themselves only with associates, and that limits their ability to create cognitive dissonance for growth. There is always someone who is smarter or is operating at a higher level than you. Find someone who has already done what you want to do in your life and hire them. Why reinvent what someone has already figured out?

I remember how foreign hiring a coach felt to me the first time. It felt so weird. None of my friends ever did that. Then I realized while none of my friends had coaches, the people who were actualizing similar dreams to mine all had coaches. If you do what successful people do, you'll get what successful people have. Previous to having a coach, I thought it was cool to make six-figures working 22 days a month until I discovered that a mentor of mine was making that amount working 12 days a month. Once I learned how to make six-figures working 12 days a month, I found a coach who only works about 5 days a month! If you want to continue to grow, you need to expand your circles to include people who have done what you want to do.

You can find a personal or business coach on websites like *www.lifecoachhub*.com or even *Thumbtack.com*. I recommend finding a coach who has already done what it is you want to accomplish. You don't need a fitness coach who has never had to lose weight or struggled with eating. Instead, you want a coach who was overweight and struggled for years and then figured out how to become healthy. Why not call your TV provider and pause your cable bill for 90 days and use the money to hire a life or business coach? What's the worst that would happen? You would watch less TV and possibly develop a new relationship with a successful person. All successful people have mentors. Having a mentor creates cognitive dissonance for what you want and convince your "horse" that you are serious. Relationships have a way of moving our subconscious mind and even igniting our will power. If 9 out of 10 of your friends are broke, you're about to be the 10th. Make sure you have mentoring relationships with successful people as it will accelerate your success and streamline your road to high self-esteem.

The next relationship you want to have is an associate. This is someone who is "in the same boat as you." This could be someone with similar goals and struggles or a business acquaintance in another market. The purpose of this relationship is to create accountability and motivation without intimidation. You'll find that when you are down, the other person can lift you up with empathy and understanding.

Join a mastermind group or an online community of people who have similar goals and have not yet achieved all of them. What's great about this is you may find future mentors as people tend to develop at a different pace than you. Be sure not to become an enabling partner who supports unproductive and negative thinking. Commit to encourage one another and hold each other accountable. It can be as simple as a weekly phone call check in or even a text. One question from an associate at the right time can be all that you need to experience a breakthrough. Just knowing my associate would call every Wednesday and ask if I completed a task was enough to motivate me to finish what I said I would do. This should also be a mutually beneficial relationship. You don't want to become a leech who does not contribute equally. While the mentor leads you, the associate walks with you. Lastly, you need a protégé or someone who is where you used to be but has expressed a desire to grow.

### The Benefits of Having a Protégé

When you teach someone else there are many mutual benefits.

First, it meets your need to contribute to others, which creates perpetual joy.

Second, it reinforces your knowledge as the teaching process causes repetition, and repetition is the key to becoming unconsciously competent.

Third, it builds your self-esteem because any time you're helping someone else your self-image is that of a teacher and mentor.

When you are willing to share what you know for someone else's benefit, the law of reciprocity will return to you more than you gave. Luke 6:38 states it this way, "Give, and it'll be given unto you, pressed down, shaken together and overflowing." Having a protégé is especially helpful during times of struggle. Most people isolate themselves and create negative self-talk during a struggle, but if you are mentoring someone, you'll find that you are teaching and motivating yourself in the process. When you hear your positive words toward your protégé, you'll reinforce your belief in yourself and your purpose. It is not difficult to find people who need what you have.

## Production

Passion plus profession are only two parts of purpose. The third P is production. There have been seasons in my life where I have done things that I have been passionate about. I also developed skills and become excellent in these areas that I am passionate about, but those are still only two-thirds of my purpose. Don't settle for two-thirds of a life. You can love to sing and be good at it but without production, you're not operating in your ultimate purpose. At best, you're just singing in the basement, and it is not blessing anyone else.

If the sum total of all of your success is self-centered, then you have missed your purpose. Let's say I'm operating in my passion—that is, I love what I do and feel compelled to do it regardless of income. Next, I get really good at my passion, and I develop my skills (that's the second P: profession) to new heights, if I do not benefit others I'm not truly in my purpose. The sum total of your passion and professional skills need to benefit others. Miserable starts with miser, and if you're miserly when it comes to sharing your skills with others, you will be miserable. To maintain the three C's of happiness: community, contribution and continuing development, our purpose needs to contribute to others in a meaningful way. This is a huge mistake that many entrepreneurs make in developing their business and life.

Do you remember the former owner of the Seattle Seahawks mentioned in chapter two? He believed he was not happy because he didn't have the right "stuff." It was only after he learned to benefit others through fulfilling his purpose, that he experienced lasting joy. It feels good for a moment to buy a new car or home, but it soon becomes a source of stress because the temporary high of a "new toy" quickly fades away when the reality of lasting happiness is not achieved. Don't get me wrong, I enjoy nice things, but they are not the source of perpetual happiness in my life. The things I've done for others continually build my self-esteem, sense of value, and increase my joy daily. The goal in life is not to accumulate the most toys but to accumulate a trail of contribution that will impact others for generations to come.

### Johnny the Bagger

A large grocery store chain trained their employees in the area of exceptional customer service. There was a bagger in one of the stores named Johnny. Johnny has Downs Syndrome. Johnny said, "I like what I heard today!" He went home and came up with an idea to impact his customers. Every night he would find a positive thought for the day. Sometimes he couldn't find one he liked, so he just made one up. His dad would help him type the positive notes and print dozens of copies. Johnny would personally sign each note and place one "thought for the day" on every person's groceries.

Notice the process. Johnny liked to make people feel good (passion). He became efficient in finding thoughts for the day and sometimes created them himself (profession). He did something that was focused on others (production).

The result of Johnny operating in his passion was astounding. One day, the store manager walked through the checkout area and the line at Johnny's register was three times longer than any other line. The manager went ballistic! He started paging cashiers to open more registers, but the customers wouldn't change lanes! They kept telling the manager "we want the thought for the day." One customer told the manager she used to shop once a week, but now she stops in and buys something every time she drives by because she wants the "thought for the day."

Three months later, each department was inspired by Johnny to create habits of Purpose that impacted both their customers and coworkers; that's leadership.

Notice, the other departments wanted to do the right thing. They were led by a boy who bags groceries. They were inspired and became self-motivated. Do you have as much capacity to lead your team? Management is using power to manipulate, but leadership is using influence to inspire motivation.

## Failure: The Event that Precedes Success

It's in your flaws, the crap, and the pain that motivates people to move towards their purpose. Every great success story is preceded by a series of failures or shortcomings, but the one common denominator is this: the person does not quit. The fact is the more pain in their lives, the more power they have. The common denominator is they embraced their pain and shortcomings and kept moving forward. Johnny the bagger's story demonstrates this. I believe it's because of his "short comings" that he was so inspirational. Once you grasp this, you will interpret all of your "negative" past events as power for your purpose. Here are some examples of "failures" that never quit and became powerful in their purpose.

### J.K. Rowling

At one point, Rowling was an unemployed and depressed single mother who never thought she would make it anywhere. She spent countless nights in coffee shops scribbling out her idea for a novel about wizards, and describes herself then as "the biggest failure she knew." (That's quite a bold statement from someone so wildly successful today.) Ultimately, it was this "failure," and the way she embraced it, that formed the foundation of her success.

She emphasized this in a commencement address she gave at Harvard University in 2008: "Failure meant a stripping away of the essential. I stopped pretending to myself that I was anything other than what I was, and I began to direct all my energies to finishing the only work that mattered to me. Had I really succeeded at anything else, I might never have found the determination to succeed in the one area where I truly belonged. I was set free, because my greatest fear had been realized, and I was still alive...and so rock bottom became a solid foundation on which I rebuilt my life."

### Sir Richard Branson

Most know Richard Branson as the iconic and daring entrepreneur and self-made billionaire who challenged established businesses by providing better services and products to consumers. It wasn't always this way.

Branson dealt with dyslexia as a child and performed poorly in school. In fact, on his last day, his headmaster told him he would either end up in prison or become a millionaire. He was almost right. Branson wasn't just successful because of his drive to prove everyone wrong. He also refused to let failure keep him from getting back up and moving forward. Some of Branson's failed ventures include: Virgin Cola, Virgin Clothes, Virgin Money, Virgin Vie, Virgin Vision, Virgin Vodka, Virgin

Wine, Virgin Jeans, Virgin Brides, Virgin Cosmetics and Virgin Cars.

The key lesson here for anyone facing challenges in life is to be resilient, persistent, and constantly looking forward to learning from mistakes.

## Nick Vujicic

The adorable Nick was born with tetra-amelia syndrome, a rare disorder characterized by the absence of all four limbs. Nick struggled with this disability during his childhood years. It was only when he came to terms with his condition that he viewed his disability as an opportunity.

Nick, at the age of 17, started a non-profit organization called *Life Without Limbs*. Nick has written four inspirational books. He is a motivational speaker who has been paid to speak all over the world; he is also married and has a daughter. You can get inspired every morning by Nick in 60 seconds a day. Just go to www.youtube.com and search motivational minute. Or see Nick's site www.lifewithoutlimbs.com

## Stephen King

Stephen King's first novel was rejected 30 times. If it weren't for King's wife, "Carrie" may not have ever existed. After being rejected by numerous publishing houses, King gave up and threw his first book in the trash. His wife, Tabitha, retrieved the manuscript and urged King to finish it. Now, King's books have sold over 350 million copies and have been made into countless major motion pictures.

## Paul's Story

My friend Paul is a Vietnam Veteran, who had a near-death experience recently. In fact, he was clinically dead for several minutes. Paul and I used to work together in a job where I was operating in my skill but not my passion. In other words, I wouldn't have shown up to that job if they weren't paying me. Although we haven't worked together in several years, Paul knows that I now speak and teach on purpose and motivation, so he called me to describe his recent death experience.

Paul started by telling me about some of the things he has lived through: an RPG hitting his helicopter in Vietnam, carrying wounded bodies, watching for the enemy in a two-man foxhole—the kind of stuff that would make for a great action movie. He thought he knew what life was about, but a few months ago he came face to face with his own mortality.

Through tears, Paul described the only thing he remembers from dying on the hospital table. He told me a voice gave him very simple instructions to bring back to earth. Paul shared that God told him we should "love and take care of each other." Many people blame their Creator for the lack of love and support. Paul told me that's what God enables us to do: love and support.

The sum total of your life should benefit others. Take care of each other. Love each other. This is the key to happiness, peace and purpose.

## It's Hard to Steer When you're Not Moving

Failure is an event, not a person so the only time failure becomes a negative is when you quit! All other failures are just resistance training, which creates the muscle to carry the purpose that is your destiny.

Do you believe that you're the creator of all things, and that you personally determine what succeeds and what fails? I don't believe that I'm the Almighty; that belief frees me up to keep moving forward. It's not my job to determine when my purpose is fulfilled. It's my job to keep moving towards it.

Have you ever tried to steer a car while the car is stationary? It's a lot more difficult especially if it has no power steering assist. Life is a lot like that. The ones who move closer to their purpose are the ones who are moving! What's holding you back? Most of the time it's a fear-based emotion; remember, fear-based emotions are unproductive.

I want to help you put it all together with some of my favorite personal development tools and processes. They key is, you have to get moving. Do it! In five years you will be five years older, but whether you're better or not is up to you. Remember, be 100% committed to something, or you will be committed to become nothing.

## Putting it Together

In order to lock in the GPS for your life you must install a destination. Imagine it's five years from now and everything in every area of your life went perfectly once you read, and implemented the five keys I've shared with you. You accomplished all of your goals, and life is going great. Can you imagine that? If not, you may have a block that may require therapy or coaching.

On the *Stress to Success Action Steps* page that follows, write down your perfect scenario five years from now. This will become the framework for the roadmap of your life. Be specific. Some like the SMART goals model, which stands for Specific, Measurable, Attainable, Realistic and Time bound. I'm okay with the SMART goals model for short-term goals, but I personally believe we should not make long-term goals from a limited (attainable/realistic) mindset. Most goals are not realistic or attainable until they are achieved.

Write down specific answers to all seven areas of your life. Remember, this is from the perspective of five years from now, if everything went perfectly. Then create a *why* for each goal. Your *why* has to be specific and meaningful to you, or you will not be operating in your purpose.

# Stress to Success Action Steps

*Create purpose goals in 7 areas of your life. Make it stick!*

## FINANCIAL

WHAT: Income, savings & investments, debt reduction, credit
*(Examples: By 20XX, I will be earning $xx a month in pre-tax income. By June 30, 20XX, I will make the last mortgage payment on the house. On September 1, 20XX, I will begin saving $85/month for my child's college tuition.)*

WHY:
*(Examples: So ____ can quit his/her job and stay home with ____. So we can be debt-free after 25 years of credit slavery. To give ____ the best start for his future career.)*

## CAREER/BUSINESS

### WHAT: New job, top producer, self employed

*(Examples: I will start my own consulting business by September 1, 20XX. I will develop at least ten clients for MY business by December 1, 20XX. I will find a financial partner to invest at least $XX by June, 20XX.)*

### WHY:

*(Examples: I want to own my own firm. I want to be free to earn as much as possible. I want to expand my business)*

## FREE TIME/FAMILY TIME

**WHAT:** Days off, vacations, trips, hobbies

*(Examples: I will take 3 weeks' vacation. We will travel to Europe. I will get my private pilot's license)*

## WHY:

*(Examples: My children are only young for a few more years. I have not spent enough quality time with my wife. It's always been a dream of mine to fly my own airplane.)*

## HEALTH/APPEARANCE

**WHAT:** Lose weight, more energy, healthier diet
*(Examples: I will be at my ideal weight of 195 lbs. I will get laser eye surgery. I will be off all prescription medications for blood pressure.)*

**WHY:**
*(Examples: I will feel great. I will look great. Prescription meds are not a sustainable future.)*

## RELATIONSHIP GOALS

**WHAT:** Family, mentors, business

*(Examples: I will re-establish communication with my cousin by September. I will approach \_\_\_\_ about providing referrals. I will begin holding staff trainings every week.)*

**WHY:**

*(Examples: I need to forgive in order to grow. \_\_\_\_ will be a great partner to accomplish my business goals. My staff will be empowered and lower my stress.)*

## PERSONAL GROWTH

**WHAT:** Education, spiritual growth, therapy, training
*(Examples: I will attend a Microsoft Excel seminar. I will sign up for Financial Peace University at my church. I will join a 21-day Fix group.)*

**WHY:**
*(Examples: I use Excel all the time and this will increase my ability and save time daily. Being debt-free will support all my other goals. Having accountability keeps me on track.)*

## MAKING A DIFFERENCE

**WHAT: Charity, tithes, mentoring**

*(Examples: I will give 10% of my income pre-tax. I will house a foreign exchange student. I will become a big-brother/big-sister.)*

**WHY:**

*(Examples: I will always receive more than I give. It builds my self-esteem to teach others.)*

## CREATE 7 IMAGES/WORDS THAT ENCAPSULATE THESE GOALS

1. Create a vision board

   Find an image or word for each of your seven areas of life. In the past, many people would use images from magazine clippings, but I like to use digital images. You may use the Internet and software like PicCollage or PowerPoint to arrange your images into a vision of your life. This is an extremely important step in locking your destination into your GPS (unconscious mind). Place your vision board in an area where you will see it often. I like to set my vision board to my lock screen on my smartphone. I often set it as my desktop image on my laptop. Some print out their vision and place it on their bedroom or office wall.

2. Visualize and meditate on it every day

   Take 5-15 minutes a day and imagine already having achieved every one of your images.

3. Use back from the future thinking

   Now that you have an image of your purpose-filled life, let's chunk it down into action steps. Remember, everything went great for the last five years, and you are operating in the center of your purpose. Now ask your "future self" these simple questions.

- How did I get it?

Using my examples, I would ask myself these questions:

- How did you lose the weight?
- How did you become a top performer?
- Where did you meet your mentor?
- What did you say to your brother to reconcile?
- How did you save the money?

## REVERSE ENGINEER YOUR LIFE

Once you've answered the "How did you get it" questions, reverse engineer your next five years. You know what you want, you know why it's important to you and you know how you got there. Ask the final question . . . when. When will you go to the seminar? When will you call your brother? When will you look into a support group? Here's an example of the whole process:

## SEVEN AREA GOALS PROCESS

- What do you want? To be at my ideal weight of 195lbs
- Why is that important? Because I'm getting older and do not want to be on meds.
- What can I do to further my progress? Ask Larry (who lost 50 lbs.) to join his fitness group
- When will I call him? *Today at 3:30 p.m.*

## DAILY MINDSET AFFIRMATIONS

- All things work together for my good
- All means ALL
- Rising up and falling down
- Every setback is a set up that moves me closer to my purpose
- I have been created for a purpose which was planned out before the beginning of time
- All of my flaws/weaknesses will be used powerfully to help someone else
- I am 100% responsible for my choices
- I cannot fail if I do not quit
- I am not responsible for the outcome, just my response
- I choose to be happy despite circumstances
- Today's catastrophes will make a great story one day

# Great Tools

### DAN'S FAVORITE WEBSITES
- Simpletruths.com: Daily emails of positivity and truth
- DarrenDaily.com: Daily Mentoring via text/email (Monday-Friday only)

### BOOKS
- *The Success Principles* by Jack Canfield
- *The Psychology of Achievement* by Brian Tracy
- *Awaken the Giant* by Anthony Robbins
- *The Seven Habits of Highly Effective People* by Stephen Covey
- *Born Rich* by Bob Proctor

### COOL APPS FOR YOUR SMARTPHONE
- Balanced: Helps you keep first things first
- Journal: Great for daily gratitude and depression
- Myfitnesspal: Keeps you focused on your daily goals
- Everydollar: Part of Financial Peace University
- Simplehabits: Set up and track new habits
- Meditation Studio: Great resource for meditation and mindset management
- Pic Collage: Create your vision board on your smartphone

### AUDIOBOOKS.COM
- AUDIBLE.COM: Greatest selection of audio books

# References

## Chapter 1: The Operating System of Our Lives

- *Self-Discipline and Emotional Control*, CareerTrack, 1993.
- Canfield, J. (2014, October 10) The Formula that Puts You in Control of Success. [Web log post]. Retrieved from http://jackcanfield.com/the-formula-that-puts-you-in-control-of-success
- http://www.sharefaith.com/guide/Christian-Music/hymns-the-songs-and-the-stories/it-is-well-with-my-soul-the-song-and-the-story.html (Hymns: The Songs and Stories) Retrieved 8/12/2016.

## Chapter 2: Perception

- Fred Astaire. (n.d.) in *Wikipedia*. Retrieved September 13, 2016, from https://en.wikipedia.org/wiki/Fred_Astaire
- [Simons, Daniel]. (2010, March 10) *Selective Attention Test*, [Video File]. Retrieved from https://www.youtube.com/watch?v=vJG698U2Mvo
- The Beatles. (n.d.) in *Wikipedia*. Retrieved September 15, 2016, from https://en.wikipedia.org/wiki/The_Beatles%27_Decca_audition

**Chapter 5: Behavior**

- Deutschman, A. Change or Die: The Three Keys to Change at Work and in Life. (2007). New York, NY: Harper Collins.
- Haefner, J. (2008, May 5) Mental Rehearsal & Visualization: The Secret to Improving Your Game Without Touching a Basketball. [Web log post]. Retrieved from https://www.breakthroughbasketball.com/mental/visualization.html
- Martson, W.M. Emotions of Normal People. (1928). New York, NY: Harcourt, Brace & Company.

**Chapter 7: The Three P's**

- Fetemi, F. The True Cost of a Bad Hire—It's More Than You Think (2016, September 28). [Web log post]. Retrieved from http://www.forbes.com/sites/falonfatemi/2016/09/28/the-true-cost-of-a-bad-hire-its-more-than-you-think/#4b738a3071e2

# ABOUT THE AUTHOR

Dan has taught how to overcome stress and increase performance through seminars all across the United States and Canada. His unique ability to connect deep psychological truths with the daily routines of individuals and organizations has helped tens of thousands change their behaviors and increase their results. Dan has gleaned from hundreds of books and thousands of articles and been mentored by the best in the personal development field. The largest seminar training organization in the U.S. frequently recommends Dan to their valued clients.

A certified personal and executive coach, Dan speaks, trains, and coaches all over the world. Dan has been married to his wife Lori since 1997 and they are raising three children near Cleveland, Ohio.

Made in the USA
Columbia, SC
30 April 2021